Handbook of Christmas Programs

Handbook of Christmas Programs

WILLIAM HENDRICKS

& CORA VOGEL

BAKER BOOK HOUSE
Grand Rapids, Michigan

Copyright 1978 by
Baker Book House Company
ISBN: 0-8010-4204-6

First printing, August 1978
Second printing, October 1979
Third printing, May 1981
Fourth printing, October 1983
Fifth printing, July 1986

"The Fullness of Time" is reprinted by permission from *Insight* magazine, copyright 1964, The Young Calvinist Federation, Grand Rapids, MI.

"A Christmas Devotional" is reprinted by permission from *Touch* magazine, copyright 1964, Calvinettes, Grand Rapids, MI.

"We Would See Jesus" is reprinted by permission from *Worship Services Using the Arts*, by Louise H. Curry and Chester M. Wetzel, The Westminster Press. Copyright © 1961, W. L. Jenkins.

"A Puritan Christmas" is reprinted by permission from *Music Makers*, © 1968 by Concordia Publishing House.

"St. Lucia's Day," "Hejom, Fejom," and "The Piñata" are from *Making Music Your Own*, Book 3 (or 4), © 1971 General Learning Corporation. Reprinted by permission of Silver Burdett Company.

The lyrics of "Christmas Is Here Again" are by G. Schirmer. Used by permission.

"By the Sea of Crystal" is reprinted by permission of the Publication Committee of the Christian Reformed Church, Inc.

PREFACE

Christmas *is* a wonderful time of the year! It is a time when we celebrate that great moment chosen by God the Father for the birth of Christ, the promised Messiah. On that first Christmas night a heavenly host burst into the darkness of human history and proclaimed, "Glory to God in the highest, and on earth peace, good will toward men." From that moment to the present, the celebration of Christ's birth has been a time of joy for old and young alike.

One of the ways we celebrate the joy of Christmas is by presenting and sharing in Christmas programs that focus on the real meaning of Christ's birth. Often such programs are presented to audiences by children of the church or school classes. Sometimes the entire church congregation participates in the program as part of the worship service; sometimes smaller church or school groups wish to use a special liturgy or series of Advent exercises as a part of the agenda of their meeting to emphasize the meaning of the Christmas season.

This **Handbook of Christmas Programs** has been prepared as a resource book for teachers or group leaders responsible for organizing and presenting such programs. The content includes a wide range of full-length programs which can be used as presented or adapted to meet the needs of a particular group. Shorter program components such as recitations, exercises, and choral readings are included to add flexibility in program planning.

Suggested designs for banners as well as models for overhead projector overlays and stage props are included at appropriate places throughout the handbook. Familiar Christmas carols may be found in a number of hymnbooks or a collection of carols, such as *The Oxford Book of Carols.* Less familiar songs from sources not as readily available are included in this handbook. A special checklist is included on page 14 to help you in your planning.

May the celebration of Christmas be a joyful experience for all who plan, present, and share in your Christmas program and through it may the name of Christ whose birthday we celebrate be honored and glorified.

William Hendricks and Cora Vogel

ACKNOWLEDGMENTS

We would be ungrateful indeed if we failed to pay tribute to the many people who have helped to make this handbook possible.

Whenever the sources are known, we have indicated them with each piece of program material. We ask the indulgence of anyone whose material has not been correctly acknowledged and ask that such omission be called to our attention so that proper recognition can be given in future printings.

We especially wish to acknowledge the encouragement of Gordon De Young, who initially suggested the project, and of Betty De Vries, whose editorial expertise has brought it to completion.

CONTENTS

Suggestions for Program Preparation 11

Part One
PROGRAMS TO BE USED IN WORSHIP SERVICES

The Light of the World 17
Waiting for Jesus Christ 24
Symbols of Christmas 39
We Would See Jesus 45
Come, Thou Long-expected Jesus 48
Let There Be Light 52
Prophet, Priest, and King 55

Part Two
PROGRAMS TO BE GIVEN TO AUDIENCES

At the Name of Jesus 61
Christmas Everywhere 67
A Night to Remember 85
He Is Altogether Lovely 90
The Pathway of Promise 95

Part Three
PROGRAMS FOR GROUPS WITHOUT AUDIENCES

Advent Wreath Programs 117
    An Advent Celebration 118
    Advent Candle Custom 122
The Fullness of Time 128
A Christmas Devotional 130

Part Four
RECITATIONS

A Child's Offering 134
That Holy Star 134
In Thine Own Heart 134
My Gift 134
A Christmas Verse 135
The Song of Mary 135
I Have a Little Secret 135
Hark, the Glad Sound! 136
The Friendly Beasts 136
The Three Kings 137
Long, Long Ago 139
Christmas 139

Part Five
EXERCISES

Christ's Birth: The Central Date in History 143

All Three Are Empty 145
How Far Is It to Bethlehem? 146
And the Word Was Made Flesh 147
Christmas Bells 148
Christmas Rhythms 149
Christmas Prophecy 155
In the Town 157

Part Six
CHORAL READINGS

Christmas Everywhere 161
Incarnate Love 163
Let Us Go Even unto Bethlehem 164
Christmas 165
A Song of Salvation 166

SUGGESTIONS FOR PROGRAM PREPARATION

ADVANCE PLANNING

Church and school leaders often begin planning for the Christmas program too late. When this happens, there is no time to follow unhurried, well-organized procedures. As a result the matter of preparing for the Christmas program may become a hectic experience, full of frustration for teachers and pupils alike.

To help make the planning and practicing for the Christmas program a happy experience for everyone, you should appoint an enthusiastic chairman and central committee in June. This early start will allow them to use the summer months to gather, review, and select the materials that best suit the talents and resources of your church or school. It will also enable them to give careful thought to the purpose, the theme, and the content of the program.

GETTING THE PROGRAM'S CONTENT APPROVED

Most churches and schools have established policies regarding the need for approval of the content of public programs to be given in their facilities or under their sponsorship. Often this is a committee of the church council if it is to be a church program or the education committee of the school board if the program is to be given in a school.

The committee responsible for planning the Christmas program should be aware of the policies and guidelines that govern the nature of programs that can be approved. Summer program planning will allow ample time to gain the approval needed before it is time to begin practice.

Keeping the minister and church council informed of program plans strengthens the cooperation among all persons involved in presenting Christmas programs in the church. Such cooperation is also needed in the case of the school program where the music teachers, classroom teachers, and school administrators work together for program success.

Approval for building use is also needed in some cases. Reserving the building early for the date of your program will avoid any possibility of schedule conflicts with weddings in churches or athletic activities in schools.

Keeping the building custodian informed of your plans and facility needs should not be overlooked.

SETTING THE PROGRAM DATE

Setting the date and time when the Christmas program will be given seems like a simple matter; and in some churches and schools this is the case, for the committee can simply agree on a date and time that seems best and announce this information a few weeks before the event is to take place.

In many communities, however, the calendar is crowded with a wide range of church and school events during the Christmas season. When you add the many family gatherings and public concerts, the calendar becomes even more crowded.

Parents and grandparents of the children who participate in your program will want to attend. The members of your church or school society will give high priority to attending the Christmas program of their church or school. Announcing the date and time of your program early will enable them to plan family gatherings and other activities in such a way that they will keep your program date clear. And this, of course, will insure a better attendance at the program.

You should have the date and time for your Christmas program set and included on the calendar of events of your church or school during the early part of the month of September.

DIVISION OF LABOR

After the planning committee members have selected materials and gained approval of program content, they need to work with teachers in the selection of program participants. Those who know the students best can make the soundest decisions as to which students will be effective narrators and which students can handle leading roles in exercises or musical numbers.

Assigning certain segments of the program to a given class or division (such as primary or intermediate) facilitates program practice. It also promotes cooperation among those members of the teaching staff responsible for a given group of children and segment of the program.

The planning committee ought also to list all matters of concern regarding the practice and presentation of the program. This list should be reviewed and the persons responsible for each item should be clearly designated. For example, if programs need to be printed, if stage props need to be built, or if posters or announcements need to be distributed, the program planning committee can delegate such tasks to others. Involving volunteers will generate more enthusiasm for the program.

PRACTICE SESSIONS

In October pupils should begin learning the songs they are to sing in the program by using them as part of their opening exercises in their classes. The Bible passages and other speaking parts can also be incorporated into the instructional program and learned by the children as a group. Integrating the songs and Bible passages into the instructional program during the pre-Christmas season will add both motivation to the instructional program and richer meaning to the Christmas program. In this way the students can master the words and music before the program is practiced in total form. Learning the speaking parts as a group will also provide many ready substitutes if the child selected to present a part in the program becomes ill at the last moment. Sending copies of the words of songs and exercises home with the children will enable parents to help the children learn them.

If the program uses one or more narrators to carry the program theme, one adult who is not simultaneously responsible for a class of children should be assigned to coach the narrators on expression and timing.

During the month of November, the songs and program parts that have been mastered by individual classes should be joined by practicing as divisions or groups. This will give the singers and speakers added confidence through presenting their parts to a slightly larger audience without the group being so large that it becomes overwhelming.

In December, the total program must be fit together. The number of total program practices should be limited to a very few in the weeks just prior to the time the program is to be rendered publicly. Having too many practices tends to make the program boring to the students participating and having too few keeps the program from going as smoothly as desired. The judgment of the teachers is the best measure of how many practice sessions are needed.

The following schedule could be used as a guide:

October: Assign and distribute long speaking parts.

Introduce songs to individual classes and begin practice.

November: Assign shorter speaking parts and exercises and begin practice.

Have individual classes continue their practice of songs and make sure the speakers with long parts are getting near to mastery.

Have several classes join together for practice of their segments of the program.

December: Continue work on individual and group parts. Include total program practices as needed.

STAGE AND SOUND SETTINGS

To enjoy a program, the audience must be able to see and hear the performance.

Arrange the stage setting and seating arrangement to simplify the movement of pupils whenever possible. For example, a speaking choir could be in one wing of the front area. The speakers could stand when speaking and be seated when they are not. To have them simply sit down when their part is completed avoids the distraction and time loss caused by having them move up to the platform and down again.

Letters or posters as well as other stage props should be large enough to be clearly seen by the audience.

The electronic sound system of the auditorium is important to the success of the program. Microphones that are spaced and adjusted properly can pick up the soft voices of the children and make them easily audible. Children generally are not accustomed to speaking into microphones and must often be shown how to do so. The sound system should be used for the final practice session as well as for the program itself in order that its effectiveness can be tested.

If no electronic sound system is available, you will need to choose children with strong voices to carry the leading parts. Using more group speaking rather than individual voices may be a good choice. Also, it may be helpful to use more singing and less speaking.

CHRISTMAS PROGRAM PREPARATION CHECKLIST

As preparation for your Christmas program progresses, check the items on the list as you complete them. Use the blank lines at the bottom for additional items that may apply to your particular situation.

_____ Appoint a program chairman and planning committee in June.

_____ Review materials and select program theme, content, and structure during the summer months.

_____ Obtain approval of program plan and content from appropriate governing authorities.

_____ Establish date and time of program and place it on church or school calendar in early September.

_____ Arrange for planning committee to meet with teaching staff in late September or early October to begin implementation of program plans.

_____ Assign long speaking parts and songs and begin practice with individual persons and classes in October.

_____ Assign shorter speaking pieces and exercises and begin practice in November.

_____ Have groups of classes hold joint practice sessions in November.

_____ Hold total group practices during December prior to program date.

_____ Contact song director and accompanist.

_____ Make building reservations.

_____ Prepare stage props.

_____ Check sound system.

_____ Clarify seating arrangements.

_____ Contact ushers.

_____ Print programs.

_____ Send out program announcements.

_____ Return borrowed props and materials.

_____ Send out thank-you notes.

Part One
PROGRAMS TO BE USED IN WORSHIP SERVICES

THE LIGHT OF THE WORLD
(a candlelight program)

Processional:	"Silent Night, Holy Night"

Leader:	In the beginning was the Word,
	   and the Word was with God,
	   and the Word was God.
	The same was in the beginning with God.
	All things were made by him: and without
	   him was not anything made that was made.
	In him was life; and the life was the
	   Light of men.
	
	Light is the most pervasive symbol in all our Christmas festivities. It is the theme of our worship this evening as we join in a service of praise to commemorate the birthday of our Lord Jesus Christ—the Light of the World.

Prayer:	"Thou Light of Ages"
	
	Thou Light of Ages, Source of living truth,
	   Shine into every groping, seeking mind;
	Let plodding age and pioneering youth
	   Each day some clearer, brighter pathway find.
	
	Thou Light of Ages, shining forth in Christ,
	   Whose brightness darkest ages could not dim,
	Grant us the spirit which for Him sufficed—
	   Rekindle here the torch of love for Him.
	<div align="right">Rolland W. Schloerb, 1893</div>

Song:	"I Heard the Voice of Jesus Say" (stanza 3)
Leader:	God's people of Old Testament times saw the Light at a distance. They worshiped the Light and wrote psalms of praise which are recorded in Holy Scripture. Psalm 104 is an anthem which gives homage to the Source of all light. *(This psalm, to be read by the speech choir, could also be read responsively by the entire audience.)*
All:	Bless the Lord, O my soul.
Reader One:	O Lord my God, thou art very great; thou art clothed with honor and majesty.
Reader Two:	Who coverest thyself with light as with a garment: Who stretchest out the heavens like a curtain:
Reader Three:	Who layeth the beams of his chambers in the waters: Who maketh the clouds his chariot:
Three Readers:	Who walketh upon the wings of the wind: Who maketh his angels spirits; his ministers a flaming fire:

Reader One:	Who laid the foundations of the earth, that it would not be removed for ever....
All:	O Lord, how manifold are thy works! in wisdom hast thou made them all: the earth is full of thy riches. (Psalm 104:1-5, 24)
Song:	"All Creatures of Our God and King"
Leader:	There was a man sent from God, whose name was John. The same came for a witness, to bear witness of the Light, that all men through him might believe. He was not that Light, but was sent to bear witness of that Light. That was the true Light, which lighteth every man that cometh into the world. (John 1:6-9)
	Isaiah was a witness to the people of God of his time that Jesus would come as the Light of the World.
Speech Choir:	Isaiah 42:5-9, 16.
All:	Thus saith God the Lord, He that created the heavens, and stretched them out; he that spread forth the earth, and that which cometh out of it; he that giveth breath unto the people upon it, and spirit to them that walk therein:
Reader One:	I the Lord have called thee in righteousness, and will hold thine hand, and will keep thee, and give thee for a covenant of the people, for a light of the Gentiles;
Three Voices:	To open the blind eyes, to bring out the prisoners from the prison, and them that sit in darkness out of the prison house.
Reader One:	I am the Lord: that is my name: and my glory will I not give to another, neither my praise to graven images.
Three Voices:	Behold, the former things are come to pass, and new things do I declare: before they spring forth I tell you of them....
Reader One:	And I will bring the blind by a way that they know not; I will lead them in paths that they have not known: I will make darkness light before them, and crooked things straight.
All:	These things will I do unto them, and not forsake them.
Song:	"Hark! the Herald Angels Sing"
Leader:	With our eternal God one day is as a thousand years and a thousand years as one day. God's timelessness is shown in Isaiah's prophecy of the coming Redeemer. Although Isaiah lived at least four hundred years before Christ, he spoke of His coming as an accomplished fact.
	Arise, shine; for thy light is come, and the glory of the Lord is risen upon thee.
	Jesus left no doubt in the minds of His followers that He was the fulfillment of that prophecy.

Jesus said:

I am the light of the world: he that followeth me shall not walk in darkness, but shall have the light of life. . . . As long as I am in the world, I am the light of the world. . . . Yet a little while is the light with you. Walk while ye have the light, lest darkness come upon you: for he that walketh in darkness knoweth not whither he goeth. While ye have light, believe in the light, that ye may be the children of light.

Many of our carols praise the Lord of Light and ask for His life-giving Light to shine in our hearts.

Songs: "O Come, O Come, Emmanuel"
"How Bright Appears the Morning Star"
"Brightest and Best of the Sons of the Morning"

Leader: This then is the message which we have heard of him, and declare unto you, that God is light, and in him is no darkness at all. If we say that we have fellowship with him, and walk in darkness, we lie, and do not the truth: But if we walk in the light, as he is in the light, we have fellowship one with another, and the blood of Jesus Christ his Son cleanseth us from all unrighteousness. . . . Again, a new commandment I write unto you, which thing is true in him and in you: because the darkness is past, and the true light now shineth. He that saith he is in the light, and hateth his brother, is in darkness even until now. He that loveth his brother abideth in the light, and there is none occasion of stumbling in him. But he that hateth his brother is in darkness, and walketh in darkness, and knoweth not whither he goeth, because that darkness hath blinded his eyes. (I John 1:5-7 and 2:8-11)

All who walk in the Light of the Lord Jesus Christ reflect His Light. God's Old Testament people were very much aware of their need for the Light of God to give them life and guidance to live the godly life.

Song: "Send Out Thy Light and Thy Truth"

(The following exercise can be done by a children's class or choir. Each child can hold a battery-operated candle. Children remain standing in a group to sing the songs which follow the Scripture texts. The verses should be memorized. As the children are taking their places on stage, the piano or organ could play softly one of the songs which will be sung at the close of the exercise.)

First Child: O send out thy light and thy truth: let them lead me. Psalm 43:3a

Second Child: For thou wilt light my candle: the Lord my God will enlighten my darkness. Psalm 18:28

Third Child: The Lord is my light and my salvation; whom shall I fear? Psalm 27:1a

Fourth Child: For with thee is the fountain of life: in thy light shall we see light. Psalm 36:9

Fifth Child: And he shall bring forth thy righteousness as the light, and thy judgment as the noonday. Psalm 37:6

Sixth Child: God is the Lord, which hath shewed us light. Psalm 118:27a

Seventh Child:	Thy word is a lamp unto my feet, and a light unto my path. Psalm 119:105
Eighth Child:	The entrance of thy words giveth light; it giveth understanding unto the simple. Psalm 119:130
Ninth Child:	The path of the just is as the shining light, that shineth more and more unto the perfect day. Proverbs 4:18
Tenth Child:	For the commandment is a lamp; and the law is light; and reproofs of instruction are the way of life. Proverbs 6:23
Songs:	"The Light of the World Is Jesus" "This Little Light of Mine"
Leader:	In His Sermon on the Mount, Jesus said, Ye are the light of the world. A city that is set on an hill cannot be hid. Neither do men light a candle, and put it under a bushel, but on a candlestick; and it giveth light unto all that are in the house. Let your light so shine before men, that they may see your good works, and glorify your father which is in heaven. (Matthew 5:14-16) Four hundred years earlier, while he was in exile, Daniel had visions of the future. He not only foretold of Christ's first coming, but he told of events which will accompany Christ's second coming and the glory of the New Jerusalem. He said, And they that be wise shall shine as the brightness of the firmament; and they that turn many to righteousness as the stars for ever and ever. (Daniel 12:3)
Song:	"When He Cometh"
Leader:	Isaiah also foretold the glory of the second coming of our Lord and expressed the joy and beauty of that new day which all God's people will share.
Speech Choir:	Isaiah 58:8-10 and 60:19, 20
Reader One:	Then shall thy light break forth as the morning, and thine health spring forth speedily:
Three Voices:	And thy righteousness shall go before thee; and the glory of the Lord shall be thy reward.
Reader Two:	Then shalt thou call, and the Lord will answer; thou shalt cry, and he will say,
All:	Here I am.
Reader Three:	If thou take away from the midst of thee the yoke, the putting forth of the finger, and speaking vanity;
Reader One:	And if thou draw out thy soul to the hungry, and satisfy the afflicted soul;

All:	Then shall thy light rise in obscurity, And thy darkness be as the noonday....
Reader Two:	The sun shall be no more thy light by day; neither for brightness shall the moon give light unto thee:
Reader Three:	But the Lord shall be unto thee an everlasting light, and thy God thy glory.
All:	Thy sun shall no more go down; neither shall thy moon withdraw itself: for the Lord shall be thine everlasting light, and the days of thy mourning shall be ended.
Leader:	While the apostle John was exiled on the island of Patmos he had a vision of the new Jerusalem where the Light of the World will shine in all His glory and beauty. John describes this city in the last two chapters of Revelation:
	And I saw a new heaven and a new earth: for the first heaven and the first earth were passed away; and there was no more sea.... And there came unto me one of the seven angels ... saying, "Come hither." ... And he carried me away in the spirit to a great and high mountain, and shewed me that great city, the holy Jerusalem, descending out of heaven from God, having the glory of God: and her light was like unto a stone most precious, even like a jasper stone, clear as crystal.... And I saw no temple therein: for the Lord God Almighty and the Lamb are the temple of it. And the city had no need of the sun, neither of the moon, to shine it it: for the glory of God did lighten it, and the Lamb is the light thereof. And the nations of them which are saved shall walk in the light of it: and the kings of the earth do bring their glory and honor into it.... And there shall be no night there; and they need no candle, neither light of the sun; for the Lord God giveth them light: and they shall reign for ever and ever.
Song:	"By the Sea of Crystal" (see page 23 for music)
Speech Choir:	Revelation 22:16b, 17 and 20b

	Jesus said:
	I am the root and the offspring of David,
	and the bright and morning star.
	And the Spirit and the bride say, Come....
	And let him that is athirst come. And
	   whosoever will, let him take the
	   water of life freely.
	Surely I come quickly.
	Amen.
	Even so, come, Lord Jesus!

Prayer:	"My Light! My Way!" O Thou, to whose all-searching sight The darkness shineth as the light, Search, prove my heart; it pants for Thee; O burst these bonds, and set it free! Wash out its stains, refine its dross, Nail my affections to the cross;

Hallow each thought; let all within
Be clean, as Thou, my Lord, art clean!

If in this darksome wild I stray,
Be Thou my Light, be Thou my Way;
No foes, no violence I fear,
No fraud, while Thou, my God, art near.

When rising floods my soul o'erflow,
When sinks my heart in waves of woe,
Jesus, Thy timely aid impart,
And raise my head, and cheer my heart.

Savior, where'er Thy steps I see,
Dauntless, untired, I follow Thee;
O let Thy hand support me still,
And lead me to Thy holy hill!

If rough and thorny be the way,
My strength proportion to my day;
Till toil, and grief, and pain shall cease,
Where all is calm, and joy, and peace.

                Nicolaus Ludwig van Zinzendorf, 1700-1760
                            tr. by John Wesley, 1703-1791

Recessional: "Break Forth, O Beauteous Light"

BY THE SEA OF CRYSTAL

John Vanderhoven, 1933

1 By the sea of crys-tal, Saints in glo-ry stand,
2 Out of trib-u-la-tion, Death and Sa-tan's hand,
3 "Un-to God Al-might-y, Sit-ting on the throne,

Myr-i-ads in num-ber, Drawn from ev-ery land.
They have been trans-lat-ed At the Lord's com-mand.
And the Lamb, vic-to-rious, Be the praise a-lone.

Robed in white ap-par-el, Washed in Jesus' blood,
In their hands they're hold-ing Palms of vic-to-ry;
God has wrought sal-va-tion, He did won-drous things;

They now reign in heav-en With the Lamb of God.
Hark! the ju-bilant cho-rus Shouts tri-um-phant-ly:
Who shall not ex-tol Thee, Ho-ly King of Kings?"

William Kuipers, 1933

WAITING FOR JESUS CHRIST

Speech Choir: **Psalm 100**

Make a joyful noise unto the Lord, all ye lands.

Serve the Lord with gladness: come before his presence with singing.

Know ye that the Lord he is God: it is he that hath made us, and not we ourselves; we are his people, and the sheep of his pasture.

Enter into his gates with thanksgiving, and into his courts with praise: be thankful unto him and bless his name.

For the Lord is good; his mercy is everlasting; and his truth endureth to all generations.

Narrator: Jesus came for the first time two thousand years ago. His coming was the climax of thousands of years of waiting. When the time was perfect, Jesus was born. He grew up—preached and taught—healed and cast out demons—was hated and rejected—but accomplished the goal of taking on Himself the sins of the whole world. God the Father accepted His sacrifice. Jesus died, but rose from the grave. He took His victorious place at God's right hand and sent His Holy Spirit. This marked the beginning of a second period of wating—waiting for Jesus to come as King of kings and Lord of lords! The church has already waited nearly two thousand years, but just as God's people knew Jesus would come the first time, so we also know He will come again.

Songs: "O Come, All Ye Faithful"
"O Come, O Come, Emmanuel"

Narrator: God made Adam and Eve perfect—in His own image. They lived in the beautiful garden of Eden and enjoyed the work God gave them to do. But Satan was jealous of their friendship with God and wanted them to be his followers. He told Adam and Eve they could be like God if they ate fruit from the tree of knowledge of good and evil. But concerning the fruit of this tree God had commanded: **Do not eat.** Adam and Eve listened to Satan and turned against God. They were forced to leave their lovely garden home and suffer pain and death for their sin. But before God sent them away He gave them the promise of a Savior.

Speech Choir: And the Lord God said unto the serpent: Because thou hast done this, thou art cursed above all cattle, and above every beast of the field . . .

And I will put enmity between thee and the woman, and between thy seed and her seed; it shall bruise thy head and thou shalt bruise his heel.

Narrator: Adam and Eve now had hope that one day someone would come to restore their friendship with God. As time went on God repeated His promise of a Savior to His special chosen people of Old Testament times. Abraham was one of God's special people who waited for Jesus to come. When Abraham was ninety-nine years old, God appeared to him and said:

Speech Choir: I am the Almighty God; walk before me, and be thou perfect. . . .

My covenant is with thee, and thou shalt be a father of many nations. . . .

And I will establish my covenant between me and thee and thy seed after

	thee in their generations for an everlasting covenant, to be a God unto thee, and to thy seed after thee. . . .
	As for Sarah, thy wife . . . I will bless her and give thee a son of her. . . .
Narrator:	Abraham laughed when God told him that he and Sarah would have a baby. When Sarah heard about it she laughed too, because they were both so old. But with God all things are possible! God told them to name their baby Isaac, which means "laughter."
	Several years later, God again appeared to Abraham. He said:
Speech Choir:	Abraham!
Abraham:	Here I am, Lord.
Speech Choir:	Take now thy son, thine only son Isaac, whom thou lovest, and get thee into the land of Moriah; and offer him there for a burnt offering upon one of the mountains which I will tell thee of.
Narrator:	Abraham obeyed God.
Speech Choir:	And Abraham took the wood of the burnt offering, and laid it upon Isaac his son; and he took the fire in his hand, and a knife; and they went both of them together.
Isaac:	Father?
Abraham:	Yes, son?
Isaac:	We have wood and fire, but where is the lamb we are going to sacrifice?
Abraham:	God will give us a lamb, son.
Narrator:	God did provide a lamb, but only after Abraham proved that he loved God more than anything in the world. He obeyed God even when he did not understand why God was asking him to do such a strange thing.
Speech Choir	By faith Abraham, when he was tried, offered up Isaac. . . . Accounting that God was able to raise him up, even from the dead.
Narrator:	God was teaching Abraham about the Lamb of God who would sacrifice Himself for the sins of the world and who would overcome death itself.
Song:	"Come, Thou Long-expected Jesus"
Narrator:	"Come, thou long-expected Jesus, Born to set thy people free. . . ."

(Project overlay #1)

But before they could be set free to worship in spirit and in truth, they had to learn how to worship. God taught His Old Testament people through the building and use of the tabernacle. The tabernacle was later replaced by the Temple. It was the house of God where His people came to worship Him. Each piece of furniture in the tabernacle and Temple was designed to help the people in their worship and to teach them about the Savior for whom they were waiting.

(The furniture can be portrayed with large drawings on poster board or with overhead projector pictures on a screen.)

BRAZEN ALTAR *(Project overlay #2)*

First Speaker: I am the brazen altar. I stand just outside the gate of the tabernacle. People sacrifice things on me, like cows, sheep, or goats. When a person knows he has disobeyed God, he brings an animal to burn for a sacrifice. This means he is sorry for his sin and wants to get right with God. He is asking God to forgive him. Just before the animal is burned, the worshiper puts his hands on the animal's head as a symbol of putting his sins there. The animal then dies for him.

Second Speaker: But what did all these sacrifices teach the people about Jesus?

First Speaker: They all pointed to Jesus, the perfect Lamb of God, who gave Himself as a sacrifice for their sins.

Speech Choir: Surely he hath borne our griefs, and carried our sorrows:
Yet we did esteem him stricken, smitten of God and afflicted.
But he was wounded for our transgressions,
He was bruised for our iniquities:
The chastisement of our peace was upon him; and with his stripes we are healed.

LAVER *(Project overlay #3)*

Third Speaker: I am the laver; I am made from the shiny brass mirrors used by the Israelite women. When Moses told the women to bring their beautiful mirrors to him, they did so gladly because they knew the mirrors were to be made into something special. Before the priests killed the animals at the brazen altar, they had to wash their hands and feet in me. They also had to wash themselves before they were allowed to go into the tabernacle to worship. So you see, my main job was to hold water for the people to make themselves clean to worship God.

Second Speaker: I know what that taught the people—Jesus would wash away their sins with His own blood.

Speech Choir: Come now, and let us reason together, saith the Lord: Though your sins be as scarlet, they shall be as white as snow; though they be red like crimson, they shall be as wool.

ALTAR OF INCENSE *(Project overlay #4)*

Fourth Speaker: I am the golden altar. I am made of wood covered with precious gold. One of the jobs of the high priest was to check me every morning and evening to make sure there was enough incense to keep burning all the time. God commanded that only *sweet* incense be burned on me. He wanted a sweet smell going up to Him day and night.

Second Speaker: When the apostle John was a prisoner on the isle of Patmos, he saw a vision of the golden altar: An angel came and stood at the altar, having a golden censer; and there was given to him much incense, that he should offer it with the prayers of all saints upon the golden altar which was before the throne. And the smoke of the incense, which came with the prayers of the saints, ascended up before God out of the angel's hand. And the angel took the censer, and filled it with fire of the altar, and cast it into the earth: and there were voices, and thunderings, and lightnings, and an earthquake.

Fourth Speaker: All the prayers of God's people go up to God like sweet-smelling incense. God hears all of our prayers because of Jesus our great High Priest who prays for us continually.

TABLE OF SHOWBREAD *(Project overlay #5)*

Fifth Speaker: I am the table of showbread. I also am made of wood and covered with gold. Every Sabbath day twelve loaves of fresh unleavened bread were placed on me. The following week when the new loaves were put in place, the old bread was eaten by the priests.

Second Speaker: All of this helped the people understand more about the Savior who is the Bread of Life. Jesus said:

Speech Choir: My Father giveth you the true bread from heaven. For the bread of God is he which cometh down from heaven, and giveth life unto the world . . . I am the bread of life: he that cometh to me shall never hunger.

Fifth Speaker: Today Christians eat the Bread of Life by studying the Word of God and by remembering Jesus' death in celebrating the Lord's Supper.

THE GOLDEN CANDLESTICK *(Project overlay #6)*

Sixth Speaker: I am a special candlestick. I am made from pure gold. I was not molded like some candlesticks, but I was *beaten* into shape. My job is to light up the Holy Place in the House of God. The priest lights me every night and I burn until daylight comes.

Speech Choir: Jesus said: I am the light of the world: he that followeth me shall not walk in darkness, but shall have the light of life.

Sixth Speaker: Jesus was also *beaten* for us, and He now lights the way to God.

VEIL *(Project overlay #7)*

Seventh Speaker: I am the veil. I separate the Holy Place from the Holy of Holies, the place where God sits on His throne, above the mercy seat. Only the high priest may go into the Holy of Holies once a year on the Day of Atonement. He carefully prepares himself for that special occasion, for he must be spotlessly clean and sprinkled with blood from the sacrifice of a perfect lamb.

Second Speaker: Now I am beginning to understand: when Jesus died, God tore open the curtain to the Holy of Holies from the top to the bottom. Jesus is our great High Priest who gave Himself, the perfect Lamb of God, as a sacrifice for all!

Seventh Speaker: We can now go directly into the presence of God, spotlessly clean and sprinkled with Jesus' blood, "by a new and living way which He opened for us through the veil—His precious body which was broken for our sins."

ARK OF THE COVENANT *(Project overlay #8)*

Eighth Speaker: I am the ark of the covenant. I, too, am made of wood overlaid with gold. My cover is called the mercy seat. My name means "place of safety." I safely keep three things: (1) the ten commandments—God's law, written on tablets of stone; (2) a golden pot of manna; and (3) Aaron's rod which started to grow again.

Second Speaker: God's law teaches us that we are sinners; the manna reminds us that God is faithful to His people; and Aaron's rod which budded shows that God can make something come alive again.

Eighth Speaker: God said: And you shall put the mercy seat on top of the ark.... There I will meet with you, and from above the mercy seat, from between the two cherubim that are upon the ark, I will speak with you all that I will give you in commandment for the people of Israel.

Speech Choir: The Lord is in his holy temple,
Let all the earth keep silence before him.

Solo Voice: The Lord reigneth, he is clothed with majesty;
the Lord is clothed with strength.

Speech Choir: O come, let us sing unto the Lord: let us make a joyful noise to the rock of our salvation.

Solo Voice: Let us come before his presence with thanksgiving,
and make a joyful noise unto him
with psalms.

Speech Choir: O come, let us worship and bow down:
let us kneel before the Lord our Maker!

Narrator: Jeremiah prophesied several hundred years before Christ:

Behold, the days come, saith the Lord, that I will make a new covenant with the house of Israel ... I will put my law in their inward parts, and write it in their hearts; and will be their God, and they shall be my people.... I will forgive their iniquity, and I will remember their sin no more.

John the Baptist was the prophet especially chosen to introduce Jesus to the New Testament people. John said:

Speech Choir: Behold, the Lamb of God, who takes away the sin of the world! This is he of whom I said, After me cometh a man which is preferred before me: for he was before me.... I have seen and have borne witness that this is the Son of God.

Narrator: God has a perfect time schedule for everything—Jesus' birth, His death, His resurrection, His ascension, and His future coming. He is waiting for each of His children to come to Him in faith and to experience eternal life through Jesus Christ our Lord.

Speech Choir: I Corinthians 15:21-26 and I Thessalonians 4:16, 17

All: For since by man came death, by man came also the resurrection of the dead.

One Voice: For as in Adam all die, even so in Christ shall all be made alive.

Three Voices:	But every man in his own order: Christ the firstfruits; afterward they that are Christ's at his coming.
All:	Then cometh the end, when he shall have delivered up the kingdom to God, even the Father; when he shall have put down all rule and all authority and power.
Three Voices:	For he must reign, till he hath put all enemies under his feet.
All:	The last enemy that shall be destroyed is death....
One Voice:	For the Lord himself shall descend from heaven with a shout, with the voice of the archangel, and with the trump of God: and the dead in Christ shall rise first:
All:	Then we which are alive and remain shall be caught up together with them in the clouds, to meet the Lord in the air: and so shall we ever be with the Lord.
Narrator:	I Jesus have sent mine angel to testify unto you these things in the churches.
One Voice:	I am the root and the offspring of David, and the bright and morning star.
Three Voices:	And the Spirit and the bride say, Come. And let him that heareth say, Come. And let him that is athirst come. And whosoever will, let him take the water of life freely....
All:	Surely I come quickly. Amen. Even so, come, Lord Jesus.
Song:	"Come, Thou Long-expected Jesus"

Adapted from a program given at the
Westminster Christian Academy,
Huntsville, Alabama

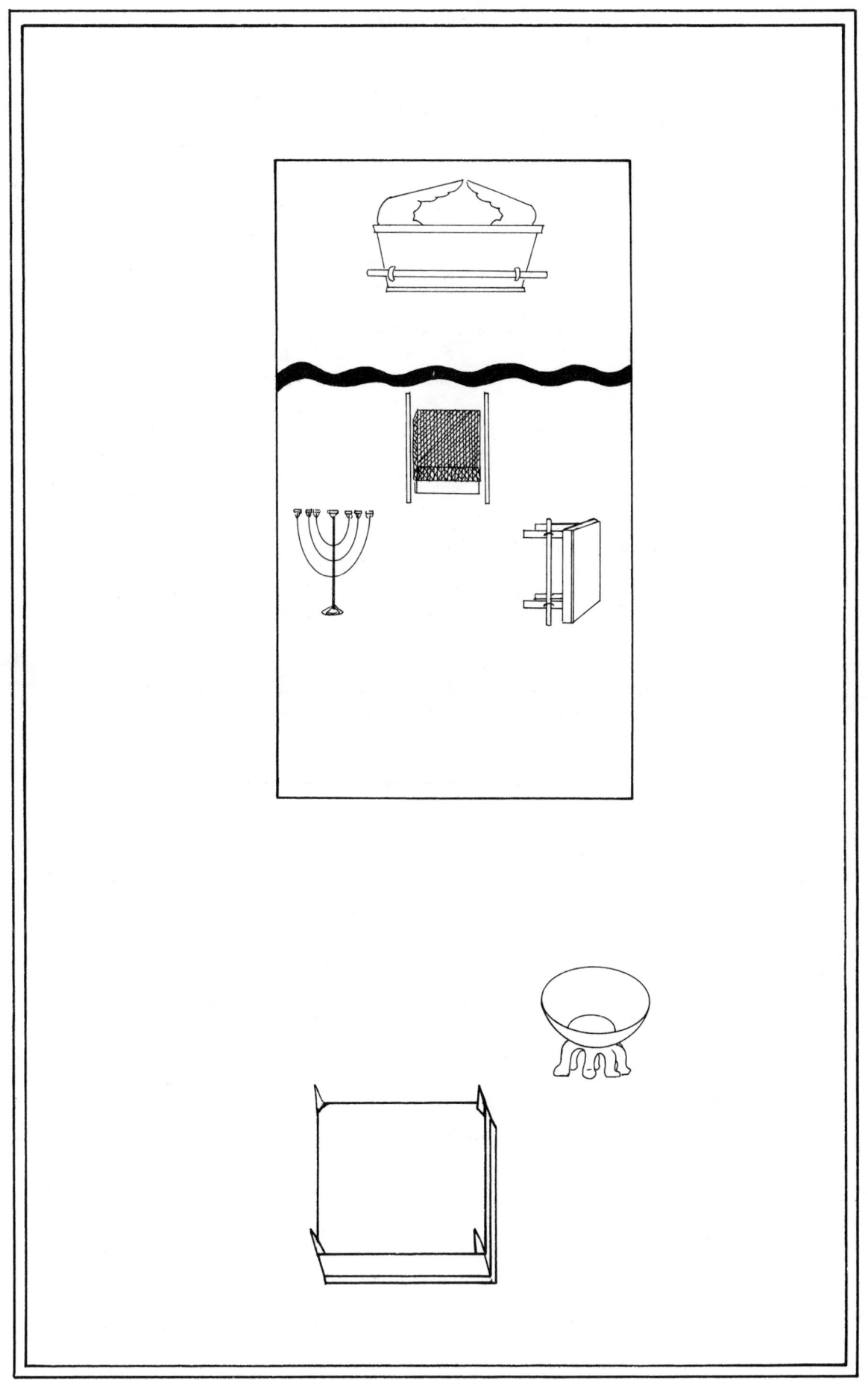

Overlay 1
THE TABERNACLE

Overlay 2
BRAZEN ALTAR

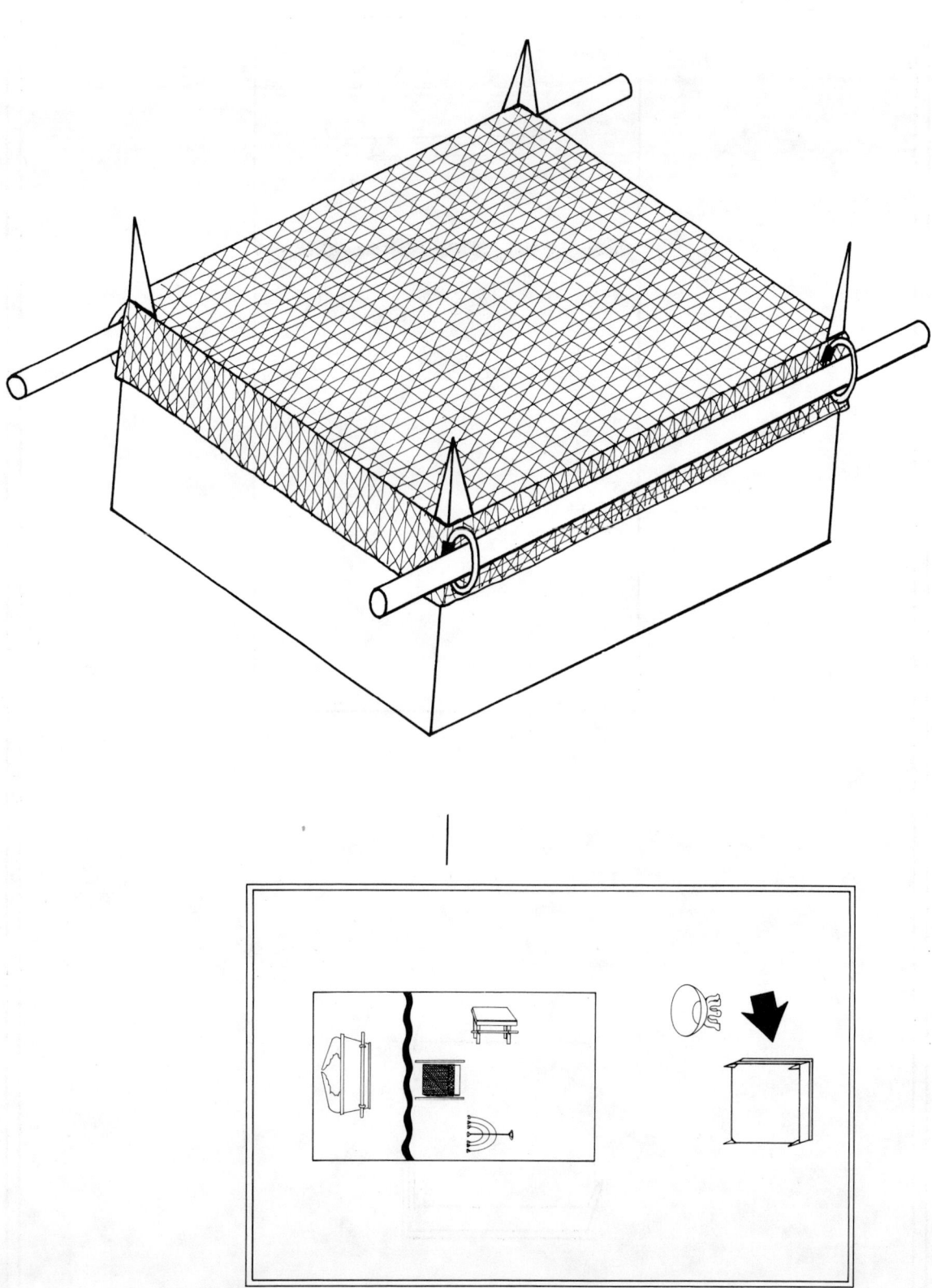

32

Overlay 3
LAVER

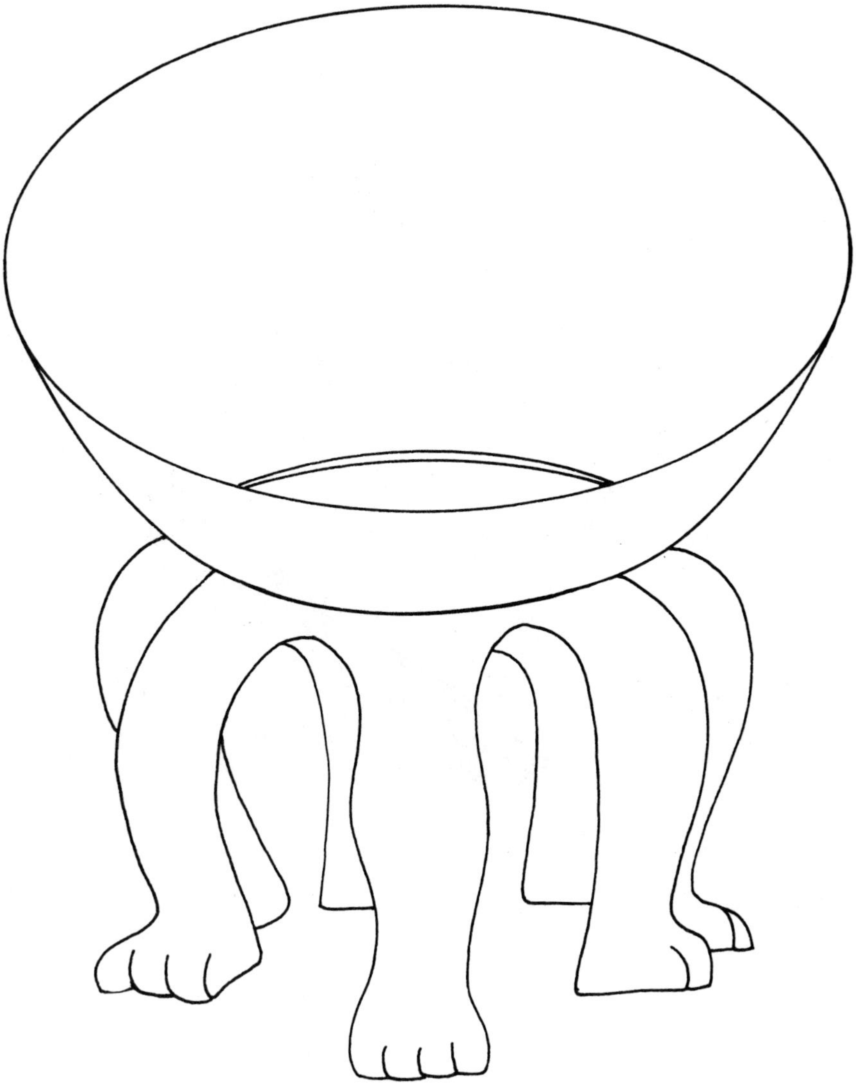

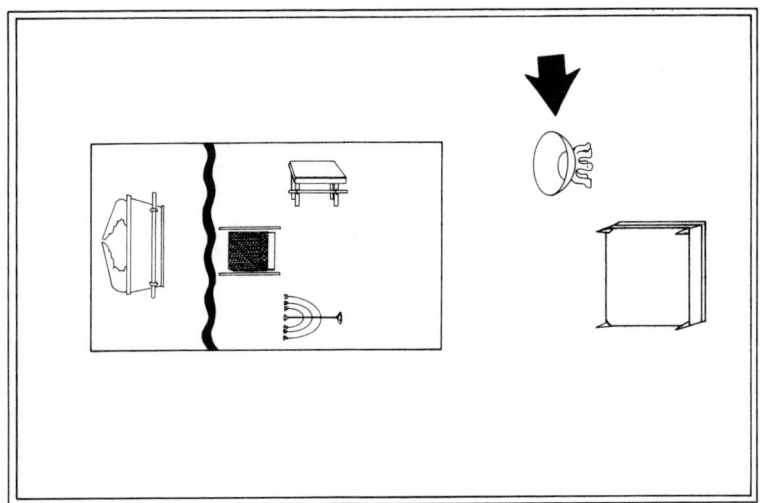

33

Overlay 4
ALTAR OF INCENSE

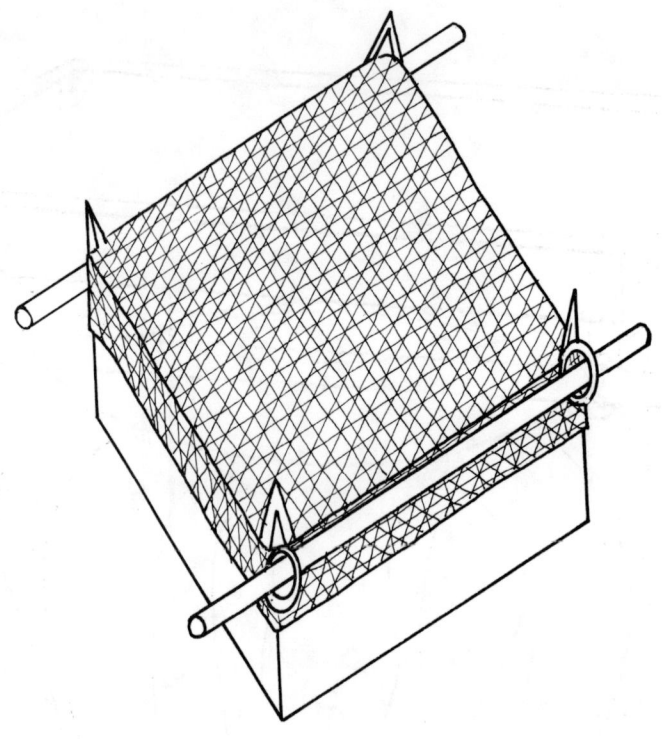

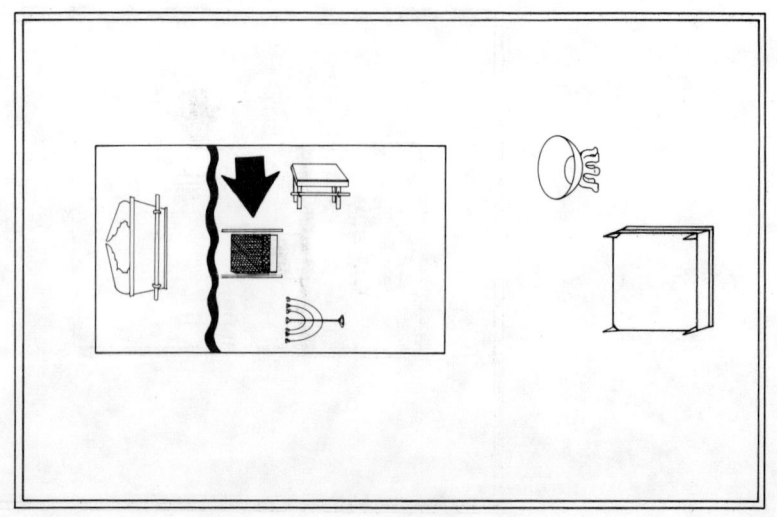

34

Overlay 5
TABLE OF SHOWBREAD

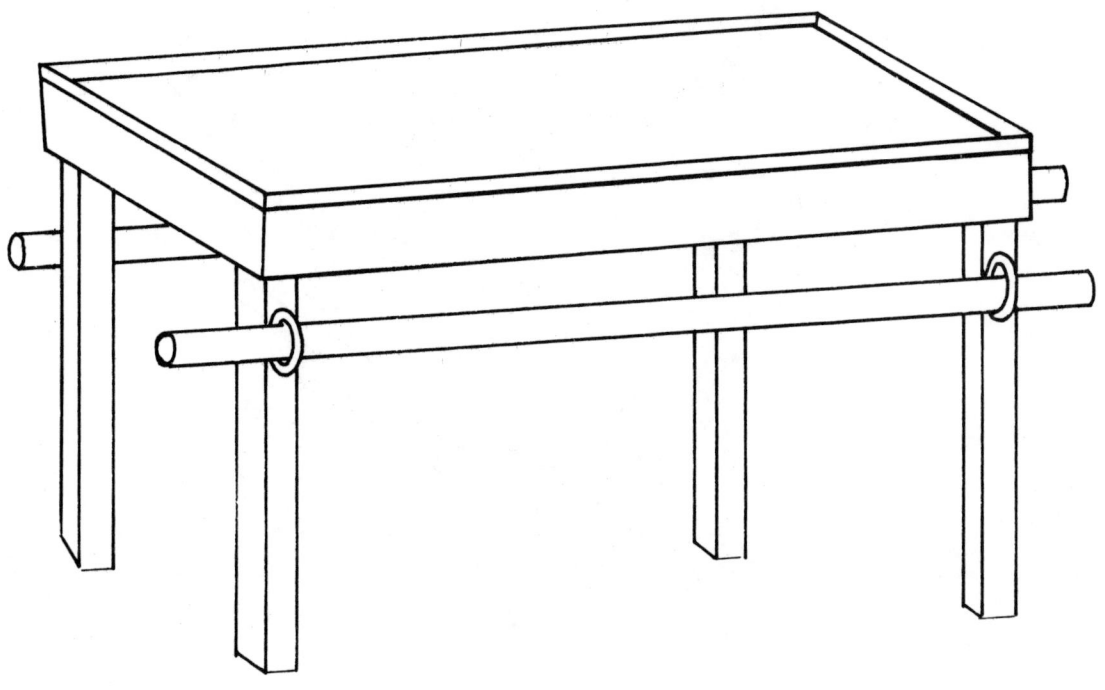

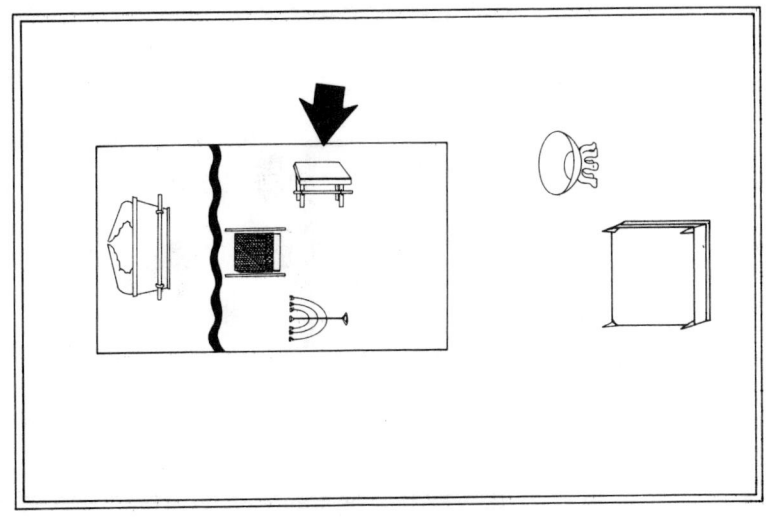

Overlay 6
THE GOLDEN CANDLESTICK

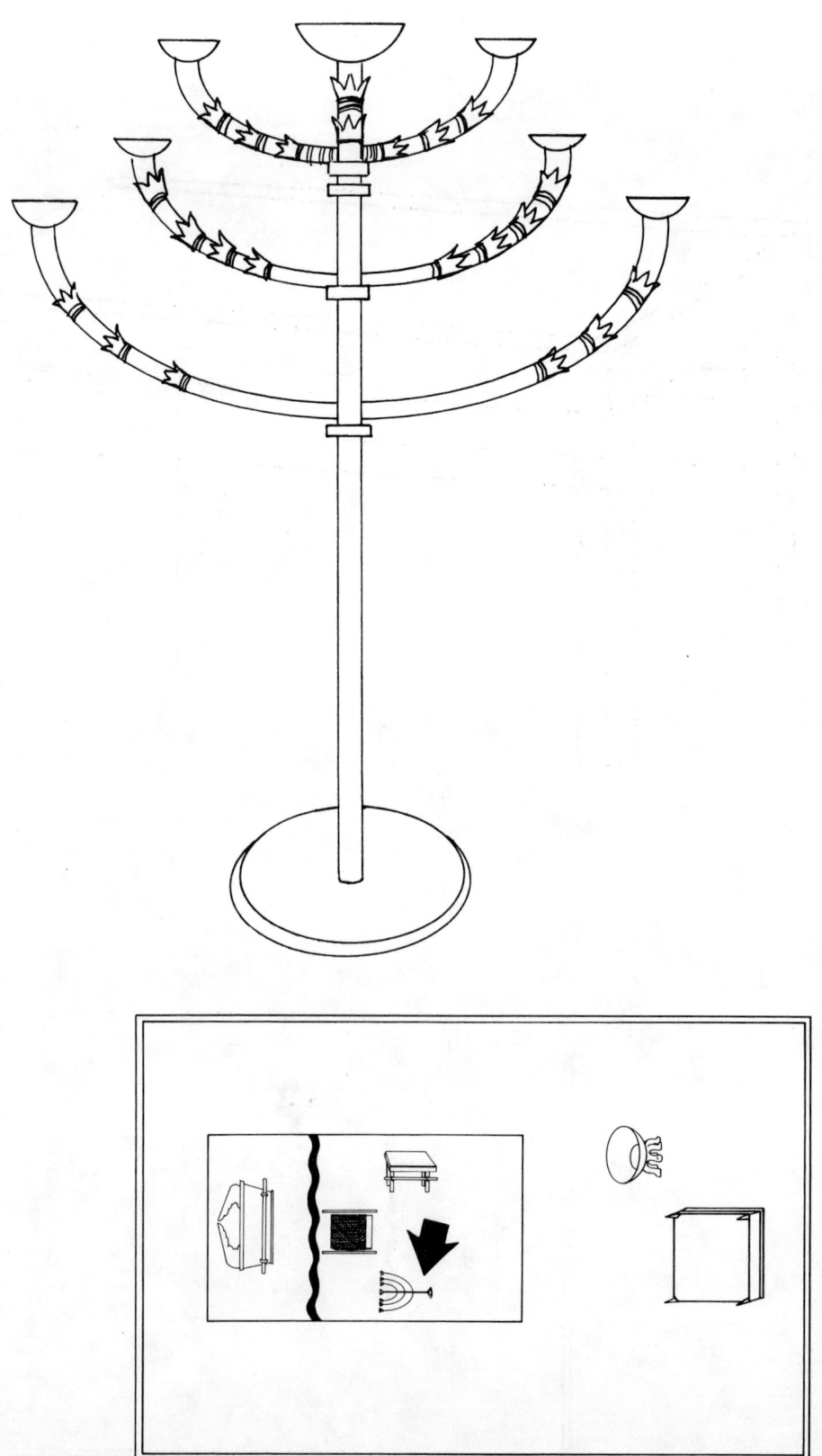

36

Overlay 7
VEIL

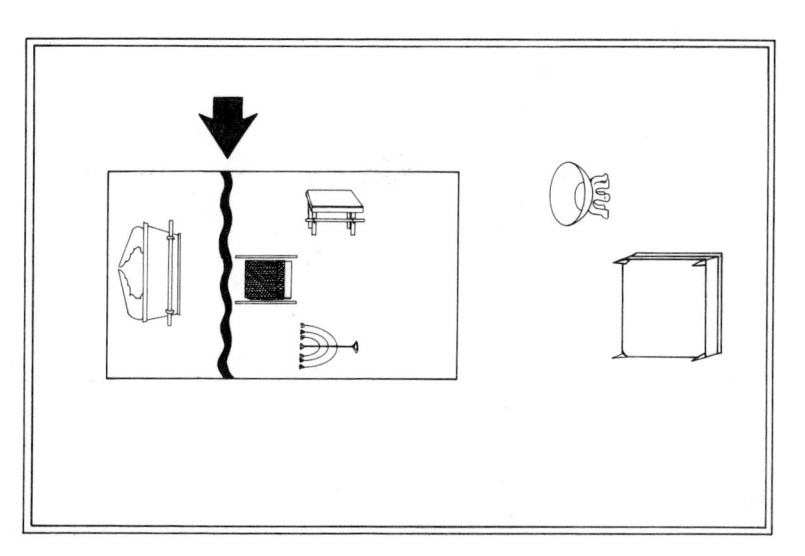

Overlay 8
ARK OF THE COVENANT

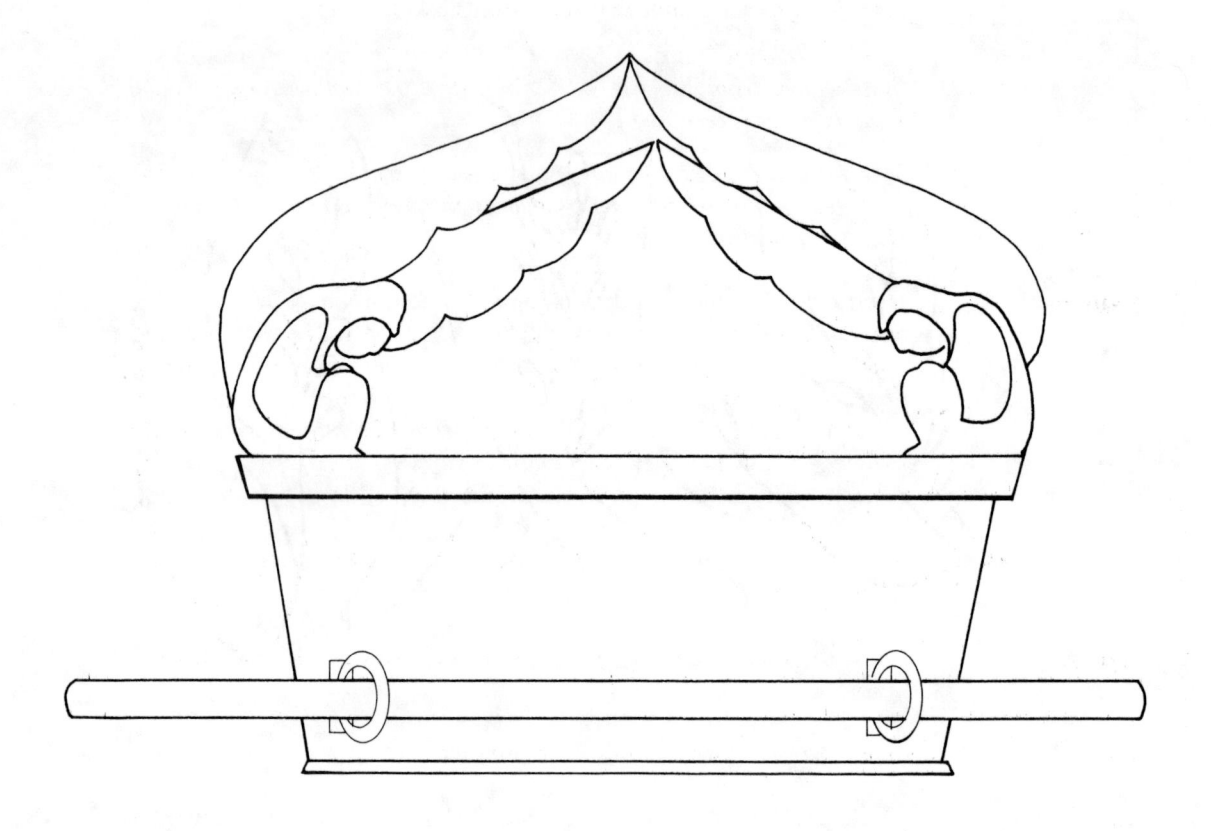

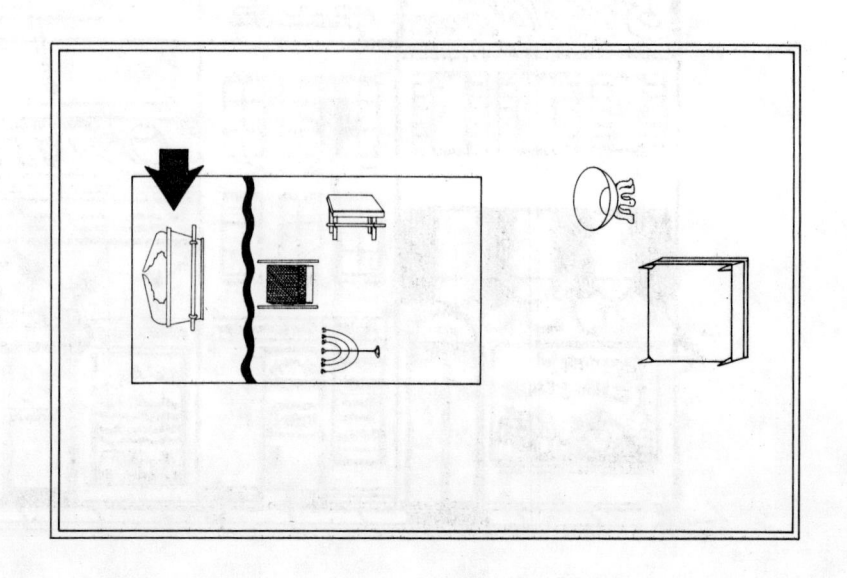

38

SYMBOLS OF CHRISTMAS

(The empty stage is lighted. The narrator is to the right of the stage. The speech choir will eventually sit behind the narrator. The singing choir is seated to the left of the stage.)

Narrator: What would the apostle John think if he came back to earth today? Let us imagine for a while that John really has come back.

(John enters from the left side of the stage. He walks slowly, looking around as if he is confused.)

(The street scene could be imaginary. Slides of real street scenes could be projected on a screen or a scene similar to the sketch on this page could be made on a stage backdrop.)

Narrator: John is on a business street of a typical American city. The streets are festooned with garlands entwined with colored lights. The shop windows display many articles which are strange to him. People are rushing about, their arms loaded with packages. Somewhere music sounds. The strains of "O Come, All Ye Faithful" and "I'm Dreaming of a White Christmas" are so mingled together that John can't tell to what the faithful are being called. It really doesn't seem to matter, however, for no one is listening.

(Children enter from left and go up on stage. They pretend they are looking at toys.)

Narrator: John comes upon some children pressing their noses against a window full of toys.

Girl: There, that's the one I wrote him to bring me.

John: Excuse me. I'm new here and confused. This seems to be a preparation for some sort of feast. Can you tell me what's going on here?

Girl: I wrote to Santa Claus for that doll. He always brings me what I want.

Boy: Don't you know nothin', mister? It's Christmas.

(The children laugh and hurry out.)

John: Christmas? That word contains the name of the Lord, the Christ. Does the festivity have to do with Him? It cannot. The children said it had to do with a strange god named Santa Claus. *(He sits down on steps to the right of the stage.)* For two thousand years people have known about my Lord. Surely all other gods have been put away!

(Shoppers enter from all sides. They don't talk but hurry on. John gets up, searching each face.)

John: My Lord brings joy, yet there is no joy in the faces of these people. I found joy in martyrdom, but these people, who are not called to martyrdom, show only worry and haste. I must find some who remember why our Lord came, some who do not worship strange gods.

(John exits as the organ plays softly, "O Come, All Ye Faithful." At the close of the song, John reenters slowly.)

John: They have forgotten. How can it be? They believe this strange god, Santa Claus, has more to offer than has God's Son. Santa Claus gives them toys, but the Christ gives joy, peace, love, and eternal life. Doesn't anyone have faith?

Narrator: John is determined to find faith somewhere!

(A woman enters holding some wrapping paper, ribbon, and gifts. She appears tired and rushed.)

Narrator: John's eyes light upon a beautiful house. There he will surely find someone who remembers his Lord, if only in gratitude.

(A knock is heard off stage. The woman pretends to open the door.)

Woman: No, don't ask me to do another thing! I've spent days in the kitchen. All my gifts are still to be wrapped. If we ever get the kids calmed down enough to go to bed tonight, we have to finish trimming the tree. No, I can't. *(She shuts the door, then stands thinking a minute.)* No, I'm not going to church. Silly, having a special service on Christmas Day. Surely I have enough to do. I can't get it all done anyway.

(The woman exits, and John turns away with a sad expression.)

Narrator: John doesn't want to hear more, because here is another person who has forgotten the Lord. On the business street again, John pauses before a shop where many bottles are displayed.

(Two men come on stage, carrying brown bags filled with bottles.)

One Man: Just making sure we have a little Christmas spirit!

(Both men laugh, yell, "Merry Christmas," and exit. One leaves by the side exit and the other down the front steps. John walks slowly back and forth across stage.)

Narrator: John saw many people drinking too much wine in his day but he is surprised to learn that two thousand years have not been sufficient to teach the world that the Christ did not come to bring that sort of cheer. John now understands why his Lord spent so much time in prayer for the people He came to save. John moves on. The search for faith seems doomed to failure, but look—he notices a lighted church.

(People walk in from left of stage; they go across the stage, down the steps and center aisle; they are smiling and appear happy.)

Narrator: People are walking briskly into the building. There is much smiling and greeting one another with "Merry Christmas." There is a spirit of friendship. John decides to follow the crowd. Surely in this group he will find some who know his Lord!

(People come up the side aisle of the church and take their seats as speech choir. John follows but sits in the front pew.)

Narrator: As John enters the church, he can hear the organ swelling in praise to God.

(The leader asks the audience to join in singing, "O Come, All Ye Faithful." The lights are turned on and the teachers enter with the children, who sit in their pews. The leader then gives a welcome and offers prayer, after which the main lights are once again dimmed.)

Narrator: The world has many signs which proclaim the Christmas season. We begin with the arrival of Santa Claus. Store windows and homes become fairylands. Newspapers, radio, and television bombard the reader and listener with merchandise available for gift-giving. Yes—worldly signs and symbols of a coming event. But we invite you to travel with us tonight back through the centuries to the beginning of time—the beginning of creation —and consider some of God's symbols of Christmas.

Speech Choir: In the beginning God created the heaven and the earth.

And the earth was without form and void; and darkness was upon the face of the deep. And the Spirit of God moved upon the face of the waters.

And God said: *Let there be light:* and there *was* light.

Narrator: This was the keynote of God's plan for men—to give men Light—a Redeemer who would be the Light of the world. And in the fullness of time, God made His announcement: high in the celestial windows He hung a star. Those who were waiting for the Savior remembered the Word of the Lord.

Speech Choir: Say unto the cities of Judah: Behold your God. For unto us a child is born, unto us a son is given: and the government shall be upon his shoulder: and his name shall be called *Wonderful, Counselor, The mighty God, The everlasting Father, the Prince of Peace.* Of the increase of his government and peace there shall be no end.... The zeal of the Lord of hosts will perform this.

Star could be projected by means of a slide or overhead projector overlay. It could also simply be imagined as narrator looks and points to the sky.

Narrator: The star—the Christmas star, announcing the birth of a King.

Singing Choir: "We Three Kings of Orient Are"

(During the singing of this carol three children dressed in colorful robes, carrying gifts, come on stage. They exit at the last stanza.)

Narrator: The star shone only at that first Christmas time. Never again has it shed its light on humanity. But man has created a symbol of that light sent by God.

Speech Choir: Thou shall light my candle:
The Lord my God shall make my darkness
To be light.
Let your light so shine before men, that they
may see your good works, and glorify your
Father which is in heaven.

Narrator: The Christmas candle, with its soft glowing flame, is a symbol of that light. In its rays we see again the light of the star, shedding its life-giving beams into the dark corners of the world.

Singing Choir: "This Little Light of Mine" or "God, Make My Life a Little Light!"

(A group of children, each carrying a candle, comes on stage for the singing of this song.)

Narrator: The Christmas bell—all the bells in Christendom ring out in joy, proclaiming the glad news that Christ is born. To us who love the Lord, these bells are a symbol of joy.

Speech Choir: *Praise ye the Lord.*
Praise God in his sanctuary:
Praise him in the firmament of his power....
Praise him with the sound of the trumpet:
Praise him with the psaltery and harp.
Praise him with the timbrel and dance:
Praise him with stringed instruments and organs....
Praise him upon the high sounding cymbals.
Let everything that hath breath praise the Lord.
Praise ye the Lord!

Singing Choir: "I Heard the Bells on Christmas Day"

(A group of children, carrying bells, comes on stage during the singing of this song. At the end of the carol they remain on stage and the other children return to the stage. All join in singing, "Away in a Manger.")

Narrator: There were no bells, candles, and colored lights that first Christmas, but down through the years the manger scene has become almost glamorous. The very straw is depicted as glowing. Mary is comfortably seated in a flowing robe of rich red or blue, and over all there is a beautiful halo of warmth. This is not how it was, for the smell of animals and earth was in that stable. Surely it was not a fit place for a King to be born! Yet when God sent His only Son to take on the form of man, He came in the humblest manner imaginable—as a baby—born in a lowly manger.

(Mary, holding a doll, and Joseph enter and go to center stage. Mary sits and Joseph kneels.)

Speech Choir: And she brought forth her firstborn son, and wrapped him in swaddling clothes, and laid him in a manger; because there was no room for them in the inn.

Singing Choir: "Once in Royal David's City"

Narrator: The manger is a symbol of the humility of Christ, a humility so deep we cannot really comprehend it. All could come to the manger; all could worship, all could adore.

(Exit Mary and Joseph.)

That first Christmas began with a family—Mary, Joseph and the Baby—all the shepherds who came to greet Him that day. Today our festivities center around the home and family of our loved ones. And what would Christmas be without a tree? A tree with tinsel and twinkling lights. Pine and balsam branches fill the room with fragrance and we gather around our trees and sing our favorite Christmas carols.

(A group of children enters; each child carries a flashlight with colored paper taped over the light. Each child is wearing a cape made of green crepe paper and sprinkled with glitter which the light will catch. They are arranged on the platform and stage in the shape of a Christmas tree. They turn on their flashlights. All other lights are turned off.)

Singing Choir: "Silent Night"

Narrator: As we exchange our gifts this Christmas, we think of that priceless gift given to us by God—the gift of His own Son, the Lord Jesus Christ.

(Some of the children turn off their lights and others leave them on in order to form the shape of a cross. All other lights remain off.)

Singing Choir: "It Is a Thing Most Wonderful" or "There Is a Green Hill Far Away"

Narrator: There are many symbols of Christmas, but most of them cannot be seen. Are you willing to forget what you may think the world owes you, and to think of what you owe the world? To close your book of complaints against God, and look around you for a place where you can sow a few seeds of happiness?

Then you are using the symbols of Christmas.

Are you willing to stoop down and consider the needs and the desires of little children? To remember the weakness and loneliness of people who are growing old? To consider the things that other people have to bear in their hearts? To make a grave for your ugly thoughts and a garden for your kindly feelings? Are you willing to do this?

Then you are using the symbols of Christmas.

Are you willing to believe that love is the strongest thing in the world—stronger than hate, stronger than evil, stronger than death—and that the blessed life which began in Bethlehem years ago is the image and brightness of Eternal Love?

Then you are using the symbols of Christmas.

This is where faith is!

Singing Choir: "Come, Praise Your Lord and Savior"

(The children exit as all the lights are turned on. John comes from his pew to the stage.)

John: My quest is ended. Here at last I have found faith on the earth.

Audience Singing: "Joy to the World"

Adapted from a play written by
Karen Van Eeuwen and Joyce Piccard

WE WOULD SEE JESUS

This simple service of worship was created by boys and girls in grades four through six. It could be presented to other groups in the church school or to the entire congregation. If it is to be presented to the larger group, it could be augmented with additional anthems and could include a Christmas story or legend, either told by an adult or dramatized.

The service of worship should be presented in a darkened room. At the center should be the screen on which the slides will be projected. This screen could be framed with scrolled wood painted gold, or it could be wreathed with evergreens. Candelabra would afford a soft light, yet not detract from the projected slides. Spotlights can be used to highlight individuals as they speak. The speaking choir should be robed in order to direct attention away from their individual personalities, and they should memorize their parts. If the congregation is to participate in the service, careful consideration should be given as to when room lights are to be turned on and off.

The color slides recommended for showing in this program may be obtained from either of the following sources:

> Rosenthal Art Slides
> 5456 South Ridgewood Court
> Chicago, IL 60615
> (312) 324-3367

You may be able to obtain these slides or similar ones at your local photography store, or a photography enthusiast from your church or school may be willing to take pictures of these paintings from art books at your local library.

If preparation is begun soon enough, the various scenes could be posed by members of your church or school, and slides could be taken of the posed scenes and projected in place of the art reproductions. This can be very effective and is often more meaningful to the worshiping congregation.

Prelude: "O Come, O Come, Emmanuel"

(During the prelude, the room lights go off and the picture **Madonna and Child,** *by Murillo, is projected.)*

Narrator: For unto us a child is born, unto us a son is given: . . . and his name shall be called Wonderful, Counselor, The mighty God, The everlasting Father, The Prince of Peace.

Hymn: "O Come, All Ye Faithful"

Prayer: *(in unison, or by the speaking choir):* Our Father, we ask forgiveness for our sins. Have mercy on us. Help us to see Jesus as our Savior, not as a warrior or a king. Help us to be good all our lives and to learn to love all people. Through Jesus Christ we pray. Amen.

Hymn: "O Little Town of Bethlehem"

(During the following Scripture and hymn, the picture **The Adoration of the Shepherds,** *by Giorgione, is projected.)*

Narrator: And there were in the same country shepherds abiding in the field, keeping watch over their flock by night. And, lo, the angel of the Lord came upon them, and the glory of the Lord shone round about them; and they were sore afraid. And the angel said unto them,

Solo Voice: Fear not: for, behold, I bring you good tidings of great joy, which shall be to all people. For unto you is born this day in the city of David a Savior, which is Christ the Lord. And this shall be a sign unto you; Ye shall find the babe wrapped in swaddling clothes, lying in a manger.

Narrator: And suddenly there was with the angel a multitude of the heavenly host praising God, and saying,

Speaking Choir: Glory to God in the highest,
And on earth peace,
Good will toward men.

Hymn: "While Shepherds Watched"

*(During the following Scripture, the picture, **The Journey of the Magi**, by Sassetta, is projected.)*

Narrator: Now when Jesus was born in Bethlehem of Judea in the days of Herod the king, behold, there came wise men from the east to Jerusalem, saying,

Three Voices: Where is he that is born King of the Jews? for we have seen his star in the east, and are come, to worship him.

Narrator: When Herod the king had heard these things, he was troubled, and all Jerusalem with him. And when he had gathered all the chief priests and scribes of the people together, he demanded of them where Christ should be born. And they said unto him,

Several Voices: In Bethlehem of Judea: for thus it is written by the prophet....

Narrator: Then Herod ... privily called the wise men, inquired of them diligently what time the star appeared. And he sent them to Bethlehem, and said,

Solo Voice: Go and search diligently for the young child; and when ye have found him, bring me word again, that I may come and worship him also.

Narrator: When they had heard the king, they departed; and, lo, the star, which they saw in the east, went before them, till it came and stood over where the young child was. When they saw the star, they rejoiced with exceeding great joy. And when they were come into the house, they saw the young child with Mary his mother, and fell down, and worshiped him:

*(At this point, the picture **Adoration of the Magi**, by Gentile de Fabriano, is projected.)*

and when they had opened their treasures, they presented unto him gifts; gold, and frankincense, and myrrh. And being warned of God in a dream that they should not return to Herod, they departed into their own country another way.

Speaking Choir:	What can I give Him Poor as I am?
Voice One:	If I were a shepherd, I would give Him a lamb,
Voice Two:	If I were a Wise Man, I would do my part—
Voice Three:	But what can I give Him,
Speaking Choir:	Give my heart.

Christina Rossetti

Prayer:	*(by the minister):* Our heavenly Father, we thank you for the birth of Christ. We thank you for the angels who sang His birth to the shepherds. We thank you that there was a place where He could be born. We thank you for the star that guided the wise men. We thank you for all the people who through the years came to see Jesus. Through Him we pray. Amen.
	(The speaking choir, divided into three groups, presents the following stanzas from different parts of the room, while the picture **Head of Christ,** *by Rembrandt, is projected.)*
Group One:	We would see Jesus, lo! His star is shining Above the stable while the angels sing; There in a manger on the hay reclining, Haste, let us lay our gifts before the King.
Group Two:	We would see Jesus, lo! His star is shining With all the listening people gathered round; While birds and flowers and sky above are preaching The blessedness which simple trust has found.
Group Three:	We would see Jesus, in the early morning Still as of old he calleth, "Follow me"; Let us arise, all meaner service scorning, Lord, we are thine, we give ourselves to thee!

J. Edgar Park from New Worship and Song
(Pilgrim Press)

Hymn:	"Joy to the World!"

From Worship Services Using the Arts by
Louise H. Curry and Chester M. Wetzel
(Philadelphia: Westminster Press)

COME, THOU LONG-EXPECTED JESUS

(liturgy for a Christmas service)

Hymn: "Come, Thou Long-expected Jesus"

THE CONFRONTATION

the setting

In the beginning God created the heaven and the earth.
And God said,
   "Let there be light . . .
     Let there be firmament . . .
       Let the dry land appear . . .
         Let the earth bring forth grass. . . ."
And God said, "It is good."

And God said, "Let us make man in our image, after our likeness."
So God created man in His own image; male and female created He them.
   And God said, "It is very good."

the fall

But by man came death.
The woman ate, and gave to the man and he did eat, and the eyes of them were opened, and they knew they were naked.

And the Lord God called to the man, "Where are you?"
   And the man said, "I was afraid, because I was naked, and I hid myself."

And the Lord said, "Have you eaten of the tree?"
   And the man said, "The woman you have given me gave me of the tree."

To the woman God said, "What is this that you have done?"
   And the woman said, "The serpent beguiled me, and I ate."

And so by man came death.

the first evangel

And the Lord said to the serpent,
   "I will put enmity between you and the woman . . .
     between your seed and her seed . . .
       He shall bruise your head, and you shall bruise His heel."

Here is the gospel in the darkest hour:
   God is not neutral; God allies Himself with man.

In this moment of confrontation the lines of battle are drawn. Behold the struggle of the seeds, the enmity that is bared:

   Cain and Abel . . .
     Esau and Jacob . . .

Moses and Pharaoh . . .
    David and Goliath . . .
        Elijah and Ahab . . .
            Two seeds . . . locked in mortal combat.

The seed of the woman is hurt; the heel is bruised; good news does not mean easy victory:

Abel lies slain in a field . . .
    The sons of God marry the daughters of men . . .
        Jerusalem is wasted and the temple destroyed . . .
            Men cannot sing Jehovah's songs in a strange land.

But the seed of the woman is not vanquished; great are the victories of the Lord for His people.

An ark rides on the waters of judgment . . .
    A sea is divided to become a way of escape . . .
        A land is conquered and divided and worked . . .
            A captive people are given release . . .
                And a ruined city is rebuilt.

But in agony of defeat, and even in the joy of victory, God's people looked for a greater revelation. Through the centuries the cry went up:

Who will show us any good?
    Where shall a man be found to redeem us?

The fulfillment was not yet; the people walked in darkness and in the shadow of death.

An expectant people cried out for God to come.

Hymn: "O Come, O Come, Emmanuel"

THE CONQUEST

the incarnation

Unpretentiously, in a little Judean town, God spoke. God, who in olden times spoke through the prophets, and in the wind and the rain and the flood
    Has in these latter days spoken to us through His Son.

The time came for a virgin to be delivered, and she gave birth to her firstborn son.
    Glory to God in the highest, and on earth peace, good will toward men.

Who is this that is born of the woman?
    His name shall be called Jesus.

What does the name *Jesus* mean?
    Savior, because He shall save His people from their sins.

the invasion

This is the day of God's invasion in the flesh.
    Hail to God's Man for men.

This day God binds the strong man, and wastes his house.
> *Hail, Lion of the tribe of Judah, God's Mighty One.*

But the kings of the earth set themselves, and the rulers take counsel against the Lord and His Anointed.
> *But He who sits in the heavens laughs;*
> *The Lord has them in derision.*

Herod the king sought the young child, to destroy Him.
> *But the wise men, warned in a dream, departed another way.*
> *And He who sat in the heavens laughed.*

Born to conflict, ordained to conquer, He spoke of war:
> *Think not that I came to bring peace to the earth;*
> *I came not to bring peace, but a sword.*

His weapons were truth and love, good words, great deeds. But other weapons were also His with which He fought and conquered.
> *Thongs twisted into a scourge . . .*
> > *Tables of moneychangers overthrown . . .*
> > > *Swine sent plunging into the sea . . .*
> > > > *Strong words: whitened sepulchres, fools . . .*

the issue

He came, the Life and Light of the world, yet often despised and rejected of men.
> *Then walked the multitude with Him no more . . .*
> > *The rich young man went away sorrowful . . .*
> > > *Then cast they Him out of His own city . . .*
> > > > *His disciples scurried into the darkness of the night.*

But there were also the moments of victory, harbingers of the final conquest:
> *Water changed to wine . . .*
> > *An adulteress forgiven . . .*
> > > *Lazarus raised . . .*

All these preludes to the final victory:
> *He is not here; He is risen as He said.*

This conquest was spoken of when the King was born:
> *The Lord shall give Him the throne of David . . .*
> > *Of His Kingdom there shall be no end . . .*
> > > *God has raised up a horn of salvation . . .*
> > > > *We shall be saved from our enemies.*

Though a babe, He was honored as a King by the angels who announced,
> *"There is born to you a Savior, who is Christ the Lord."*

By shepherds who hastened to the manger
> *And returned, glorifying and praising God.*

By the wise men
> *Who fell down and worshiped, presenting their gifts.*

By aged Simeon, who blessed God and said,
"Mine eyes have seen thy salvation."

We now, who share in His conquest, join in our praise.
Rejoice, ye heavens; thou earth reply
With praise, ye sinners, fill the sky
For this, His incarnation.
Incarnate God, put forth Thy Power,
Ride on, Ride on, great Conqueror
Till all know Thy salvation.

Hymn: "Angels, from the Realms of Glory"

Calvin College Chapel Service

LET THERE BE LIGHT

(liturgy for a Christmas service)

Choir: "Never Shone a Light So Fair"

LET THERE BE LIGHT

And God said, "Let there be light." And there was light.
And God saw the light, that it was good.

And man was blessed by the light; the light of the sun and the moon and the stars
And the light of the presence of the Lord.

And out of the darkness of hell came the prince of the principalities and powers, disguised as an angel of light, but in truth the ruler of darkness.

"Take, eat, remember, and believe that you shall be as God," he said.
And she took thereof, and did eat, and gave also unto her husband with her, and he did eat.

And it was night, and great was the darkness in which men groped
In fear and pain and death.

And men walk in the darkness, and love the darkness rather than the light.

LET THERE BE LIGHT

The words were spoken even as the first shades of night were falling . . .
"I will put enmity between thee and the woman, and between thy seed and her seed. It shall bruise thy head, and thou shalt bruise His heel."

Here is a word of light, of conflict between midnight and noon, of the conquest of the light over the darkness.

And through the days of old, men found comfort in the light.
"The Lord is my light and my salvation; whom shall I fear?"
"The Lord is a sun and shield; the Lord will give grace and glory."

Yet, living in the light, they looked for a still brighter day, spoken of by the prophets:
"The Lord shall be thine everlasting light";
"The people who walk in darkness shall see a great light."
"Unto you that fear my name shall the Sun of Righteousness arise with healing in His wings."

Hymn: "O Come, O Come, Emmanuel"

LET THERE BE LIGHT

In the beginning was the Word, and the Word was with God, and the Word was God.
In Him was life; and the life was the light of men.

Of Him an aged Zacharias declared, "The dayspring from on high hath visited us.
To give light to them that sit in darkness and in the shadow of death."

And at His birth the Judean hills saw the brightness of angelic hosts and heavenly glory,
   And shepherds returned, glorifying and praising God.

And wise men from the east came, for they had seen His star in the east, and when they saw the young child with Mary His mother,
   they fell down, and worshiped Him.

Solo: "Brightest and Best of the Sons of the Morning"

LET THERE BE LIGHT

Jesus grew, and increased in wisdom and stature, and in favor with God and man.

And all the people came unto Him, and He taught them, saying,
   "I am the Light of the world."

He walked among us, and shed His light upon us,
   and in His light we see the light.

The brightness of His presence brought light and joy to a troubled world;
   The blind received their sight; the lame walked; the dead were raised to life; and all men had good tidings preached to them.

For Christ is the Light.

Audience: "I heard the voice of Jesus say,
   'I am this dark world's light;
   Look unto Me; thy morn shall rise,
   And all thy day be bright!'
   I looked to Jesus and I found
   In Him my star, my son;
   And in that light of life I'll walk,
   Till trav'ling days are done."

BUT DARKNESS FELL

The nations raged; kingdoms were moved; rulers took counsel together against the Lord and His Anointed.
   And it was midnight, in the hearts of men and in the world.

Amidst the flickering torches and eerie shadows of the garden one came and kissed Him;
   And it was midnight in his heart too.

And the fires in the courtyard and the lamps in the courtroom could not dispel the darkness that covered the hearts of men.
   And then, from the sixth hour there was darkness over all the land unto the ninth hour.

And about the ninth hour Jesus cried with a loud voice:
   "My God, My God, why hast Thou forsaken me?"

It was midnight . . . at high noon.

Solo: "Alas, and Did My Savior Bleed."

AND THERE WAS LIGHT

At the end of the sabbath, as it began to dawn, God said,
"Let there be light."

And there was a great earthquake; for the angel rolled back the stone from the door.
"Christ is not here; He is risen as He said."

The powers of death were vanquished; the darkness of hell had been pierced.
"For by His appearing He hath abolished death, and hath brought life and immortality to light."

Choir: "Welcome, Happy Morning"

Prayer

Christ, whose glory fills the skies, Christ, the true and only Light,
Sun of Righteousness, arise; triumph o'er the shades of night;

Dayspring from on high, be near;
Day-star, in my heart appear.

Visit, then, this soul of mine, pierce the gloom of sin and grief;
Fill me, Radiancy divine; scatter all my unbelief;

More and more Thyself display,
Shining to the perfect day. Amen.

Audience: "Sun of my soul, Thou Savior dear,
It is not night if Thou be near;
O may no earth-born cloud arise,
To hide Thee from Thy servant's eyes."

"Praise God, from whom all blessings flow;
Praise Him, all creatures here below;
Praise Him above, ye heavenly host.
Praise Father, Son, and Holy Ghost."

Calvin College Chapel Service

PROPHET, PRIEST, AND KING

(litany for a Christmas service)

Christmas Lesson: Luke 2:8-11

What does the name *Christ* mean?
The Anointed One.

For what purpose was Jesus anointed?
He was anointed to be our Chief Prophet, our only High Priest, and our Eternal King.

OUR CHIEF PROPHET

God said, "Let us make man in our image, after our likeness."
And He created man, and blessed him with true knowledge.

God commanded, "Thou shalt not eat of the tree, lest thou die."
And Satan said, "Take, eat, and live."
And man took and did eat.

No longer did man know the truth of God, but stumbled along:
Darkened in understanding . . .
Ignorant of God's righteousness . . .
Listening to strange voices . . .
Hearing not the voice of God.

But where shall wisdom be found? and where is the place of understanding?
God understands the way to it, and He knows its place.

And God proclaimed the evangel from of old:
Through the deliverer Moses:
I will raise them up a prophet from among their brethren, and will put my words in his mouth.

Through the evangelist Isaiah:
The Lord hath anointed me to preach good tidings unto the meek . . . to proclaim liberty to the captives.

And through the Spirit-filled Zacharias:
The dayspring from on high hath visited us, to give light to them that sit in darkness . . . to guide our feet in the way of peace.

It is the day of fulfillment: The virgin hath borne a son.
Unto us a Prophet is born.
Prophet from God . . . Light to men
Revelation . . . and Revealer
Word become flesh . . . Incarnate Truth
Never man spake like this man:
Blessed are the poor in spirit . . .
And a Sower went forth to sow . . .
Thy sins are forgiven thee . . .
Whoso confesseth me, him will I confess.

Speak, Lord, for thy servants hear.

Hymn: "Lord, Speak to Me, That I May Speak"

OUR ONLY HIGH PRIEST

God made man in His image, holy and without sin,
   That man might give himself a sacrifice of thanksgiving.
But man took of the tree, and did eat.

Adam, where art thou?
        and it was silent.
Wherefore art thou hiding?
        I am afraid.
What hast thou done?
        I did eat.
Thou must die.
        And without shedding of blood is no remission.

To the condemned, God gave the evangel in symbol and rite:
   A ram caught in a thicket...
     A scapegoat driven into the wilds...
       A brazen serpent against an eastern sky...
     A mercy seat sprinkled with blood.

And there was the evangel in the word, the prophecy of a priest.
   He hath borne our grief and carried our sorrow...
   The Lord hath laid on Him the iniquity of us all...

It is the day of fulfillment. The virgin hath borne a son.
   Unto us a Priest is born.
Lamb of God ... Our Passover
Suffering Servant ... Man of Sorrows
Bread and Wine ... Body and Blood
For He was Born ... to Die:
   The Son of man came to lay down His life...
   And I, if I be lifted up, shall draw all men...
   This do in remembrance of me...
   It is finished.

Simeon blessed the young child and His mother, and said to Mary, "A sword shall pierce through thy own soul also."
   Now there stood by the cross of Jesus His mother.
And Simeon said, "This child is set for the fall and rising of many in Israel."
   One malefactor railed, and the other cried, "Lord, remember."

Having such a High Priest, let us draw near with a true heart.
   Let us hold fast the profession of our faith without wavering.

Hymn: "Christians, Awake, Salute the Happy Morn"

OUR ETERNAL KING

God planted a garden, and there He put man, saying,
   "Subdue the earth, and have dominion over it."

Man, king of creation, vice-regent under God, highly exalted,
Exalted himself . . . and fell.

And every man did that which was right in his own eyes:
Cain rose up against Abel his brother and slew him . . .
Lamech slew a young man for striking him . . .
The sons of God took to wife the daughters of men.
And God was sorry that He had made man on the earth.

There is none that doeth good, no, not one.
And to this no-good world came the evangel from God:
Good news of a throne and a kingdom and a King.

To the lawless and the rebel came the prophecy:
Rejoice, O daughter of Zion, thy King cometh . . .
I will set my King upon my holy hill . . .
Of the increase of His government there shall be no end . . .
The God of heaven shall set up a kingdom, and it shall stand forever . . .

It is the day of fulfillment. The virgin hath borne a son.
Unto us a King is born.
Son of David . . . Arm of the Lord
Lion of Judah . . . Blessed Potentate
King of kings . . . Lord of lords.
Worthy is the Lord to receive all glory and praise:
Shepherds feared, wondered, and rejoiced . . .
Wise men fell down and worshiped . . .
Anna gave thanks.
And what say you?
Glory to our King.

Cross and crown, these two; crown through cross, this too:
They plaited a crown of thorns
        and crushed it on His head.
They spat and cuffed and cried,
        "Hail, King of the Jews."
In three languages it was written:
        JESUS OF NAZARETH, KING OF THE JEWS.

Manger . . . Cross . . . Crown.
Born our King; dying our King; risen our King.
King He was
    and King He is
        and King He ever shall be.
Glory to our new-born King.

Hymn: "Come, Thou Long-expected Jesus"

Calvin College Chapel Service

Part Two

PROGRAMS TO BE GIVEN TO AUDIENCES

AT THE NAME OF JESUS

Organ Prelude

Welcome and Opening Prayer

Song: "Watchman, Tell Us of the Night."

(This is to be sung by a selected class or group of children who are seated in the auditorium before the program begins.)

Processional Song: "Once in Royal David's City."

(This is played by the organist as remainder of the children enter. When all are in place, the song is to be sung by entire group.)

Speaker One: God created man to have fellowship with Him. God hates man's sin, man's disobedience. But God did not allow man to be destroyed by his own selfishness. In His love, God reached out and sent His Son to save us. Jesus Christ took on our human nature; He became man to free us from slavery to sin and to the devil. This is the great story of Christmas, the story of Jesus.

(Enter students carrying the theme banner: After the banner is hung, all students join to sing.)

THE NAMES OF OUR SAVIOR

Song: "At the Name of Jesus," verses 1-3.

Speaker Two: Who is this Jesus? People asked this question on the street corners of Jerusalem and on the highways where Jesus walked. They are asking it today in twentieth-century cities and in a space-minded world.

Speaker Three: The names of Jesus tell us who He is. He has many names. Each of them tells us something great and wonderful about Him. By whatever name we call Him, Jesus is the Christ of Christmas. He it is that we have come to honor and to worship.

Song: "Jesus Loves Me."

*(Enter student carrying a banner with the name **Jesus** which he mounts on the theme banner.)*

THE NAMES OF OUR SAVIOR

JESUS

Speaker Four:	Jesus is the human name of the Son of God.
Speaker Five:	An angel appeared to Joseph and said that Mary would give birth to a son. "Thou shalt call his name Jesus: for he shall save his people from their sins." (Matthew 1:21)
Speaker Six:	The angel that appeared to Mary told her that she would give birth to a son and that she should "call his name Jesus. He shall be great, and shall be called the Son of the Highest." (Luke 1:31, 32)
Song:	"Joys Seven."
Speakers One-Six:	"Neither is there salvation in any other: for there is none other name under heaven given among men, whereby we must be saved." (Acts 4:12)
Song:	"At the Name of Jesus," verses 5 and 7.

*(Enter student carrying banner with the name **Christ** which he mounts on the theme banner. All subsequent banners will be mounted in the same fashion.)*

THE NAMES OF OUR SAVIOR

JESUS   CHRIST

Speaker Seven:	Jesus is also called Christ.
Speaker Eight:	Long before the birth of Jesus, God promised His people that He would send to earth a Savior. Through the centuries of waiting for this Savior, He was called the Messiah or the Christ. These names mean "anointed" or "chosen of God."

Song:	"Good Christian Men, Rejoice."
Speaker Nine:	"And there were in the same country shepherds abiding in the field, keeping watch over their flock by night. And, lo, the angel of the Lord came upon them, and the glory of the Lord shone round about them; and they were sore afraid. And the angel said unto them, Fear not: for, behold, I bring you good tidings of great joy, which shall be to all people. For unto you is born this day, in the city of David, a Savior, which is *Christ* the Lord." (Luke 2:8-11)
Speakers Seven-Nine:	"Whosoever believeth that Jesus is the Christ is born of God. . . . For whatsoever is born of God overcometh the world: and this is the victory that overcometh the world, even our faith." (I John 5:1, 4)
Song:	"Hark! the Herald Angels Sing," verses 1 and 2.
Speaker Ten:	The Old Testament refers to the promised Christ in other ways also.
Speaker Eleven:	He is called a star, a light, a sun!

(Enter students carrying banners made in the shape of a silver star and a golden sun which they mount on the theme banner.)

THE NAMES OF OUR SAVIOR

JESUS CHRIST ★ STAR ☼ SUN

Speakers Ten-Eleven:	"I shall see him, but not now: I shall behold him, but not nigh: there shall come a *Star* out of Jacob, and a Sceptre shall rise out of Israel." (Numbers 24:17)
Speaker Twelve:	"Arise, shine; for thy light is come, and the glory of the Lord is risen upon thee." (Isaiah 60:1)
Song:	"Hark! the Herald Angels Sing," verse 3.
Speaker Thirteen:	During Old Testament times, the promised Christ was also called Emmanuel, which means "God with us."

*(Enter student carrying a banner with the name **Emmanuel** which he mounts.)*

THE NAMES OF OUR SAVIOR

JESUS | CHRIST | STAR / SUN | EMMANUEL

Speaker Fourteen: "Now all this was done, that it might be fulfilled which was spoken of the Lord by the prophet, saying, Behold, a virgin shall be with child, and shall bring forth a son, and they shall call his name Emmanuel, which being interpreted is, God with us." (Matthew 1:22, 23)

Song: "Sing with Joy, Glad Voices Lift."

Speaker Fifteen: The Bible also calls Jesus *King.* This name of Jesus shows His authority and honors Him as ruler of all.

*(Enter student carrying a banner with the name **King** which he mounts.)*

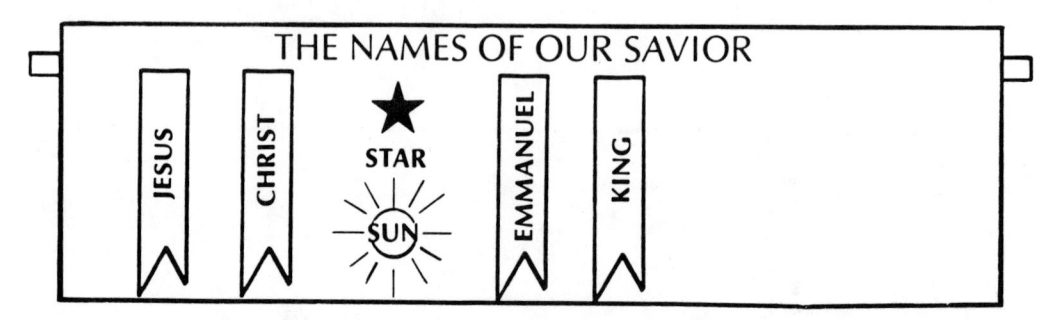

THE NAMES OF OUR SAVIOR

JESUS | CHRIST | STAR / SUN | EMMANUEL | KING

Speaker Sixteen: "Rejoice greatly, O daughter of Zion! Shout aloud, O daughter of Jerusalem! Lo, your king comes to you; triumphant and victorious is he.... And he shall command peace to the nations; his dominion shall be from sea to sea." (Zechariah 9:9, 10)

Song: "Christ Shall Have Dominion," verse 1.

Speaker Seventeen: Jesus is called the *Son of God.*

*(Enter student carrying a banner with the name **Son of God** which he mounts.)*

THE NAMES OF OUR SAVIOR

JESUS | CHRIST | STAR / SUN | EMMANUEL | KING | SON OF GOD

Speaker Eighteen:	The angel said to Mary, "The Holy Spirit will come upon you, and the power of the Most High will overshadow you; therefore the child to be born will be called holy, the *Son of God.*" (Luke 1:35)
Speakers Seventeen-Eighteen:	"For God so loved the world, that he gave his only begotten Son, that whosoever believeth in him should not perish, but have everlasting life." (John 3:16)
Song:	"God Rest You Merry, Gentlemen," verses 1 and 2.
Speaker Nineteen:	Jesus was not only called the Son of God, He was also called the *Son of man.*

(Enter student carrying a banner with the name **Son of man** *which he mounts.)*

THE NAMES OF OUR SAVIOR

JESUS — CHRIST — ★ STAR / SUN — EMMANUEL — KING — SON OF GOD — SON OF MAN

Speaker Twenty:	To be our Savior, Jesus needed not only a divine nature, but He also needed a human nature. There are several ways in which we learn about Jesus' humanness. Like any other human being, Jesus was born. Like us, He laughed and cried. He grew to be a man and lived with other people; He worked; He grew tired; He slept. But He was more than a man, for He came from heaven to be the Savior of men.
Song:	"The Coventry Carol."
Speaker Twenty-One:	"And Joseph also went up from Galilee, out of the city of Nazareth, into Judea, unto the city of David, which is called Bethlehem; because he was of the house and lineage of David; to be taxed with Mary his espoused wife, being great with child. And so it was, that, while they were there, the days were accomplished that she should be delivered. And she brought forth her firstborn son, and wrapped him in swaddling clothes, and laid him in a manger; because there was no room for them in the inn." (Luke 2:4-7)
Song:	"Away in a Manger."
Speaker Twenty-Two:	"And there were in the same country shepherds abiding in the field, keeping watch over their flock by night. And, lo, the angel of the Lord came upon them, and the glory of the Lord shone round about them; and they were sore afraid. And the angel said unto them, Fear not; for, behold, I bring you good tidings of great joy, which shall be to all people. For unto you is born this day, in the city of David, a Savior which is Christ the

Lord. And this shall be a sign unto you; Ye shall find the babe wrapped in swaddling clothes, lying in a manger. And suddenly there was with the angel a multitude of the heavenly host praising God, and saying,

Speakers
Twenty-One—
Twenty-Two: Glory to God in the highest, and on earth peace, good will toward men." (Luke 2:8-14)

Song: "Angels We Have Heard on High."

Speaker
Twenty-Three: Jesus whose birth was proclaimed by the angels is truly Lord.

*(Enter student carrying a banner with the name **Lord** which he mounts. The theme banner is now complete.)*

THE NAMES OF OUR SAVIOR

JESUS | CHRIST | ★ STAR / SUN | EMMANUEL | KING | SON OF GOD | SON OF MAN | LORD

Speaker
Twenty-Four: One of the Old Testament prophets referred to the coming Messiah as a Wonderful Counselor and also called Him the Prince of Peace. Just as Jesus was called the Mighty God in the Old Testament, so He is called Lord many, many times in the New Testament. This name tells us that Jesus is master, the ruler over all things in heaven and on earth. He is ruler over sin and death as well. O come, let us adore Him!

Song: "O Come, All Ye Faithful," last verse.

Speaker
Twenty-Five: Jesus, whose birth we celebrate at Christmas, is Lord of lords and King of kings. We marvel at God's love when we consider that He sent His sinless Son to earth to be our Savior.

Solo: "I Wonder as I Wander" or "What Child Is This."

Speakers One—
Twenty-Five: Thanks be to you, my Lord and my God!
Take my life for I would live to your praise;
Take my hands and my feet so that what I do and where I go will serve you;
Take my voice and my lips and use them to honor you;
Take my silver and my gold and help me to use them for your cause;
Take myself so I may truly live for you!
Thank you for Jesus and the joy of Christmas!

Song: "Joy to the World."

Recessional

Adapted from a program written by
Janice Postma and presented at the
Sylvan Christian School,
Grand Rapids.

CHRISTMAS EVERYWHERE

(No stage setting is required. If real flags are used, flag stands will be needed. If the flags are made from some type of poster paper, a space will need to be provided so they can be hung on a wire or wall as they are brought in.)

Narrator One: This is the season of the year when we remember the birth of our Savior. It is a time of joy and happiness. Christmas is a time for singing and celebrating, a time when gifts are given as symbols of God's gift to us, the greatest gift of all, Jesus Christ. It is a time when lights are put up in honor of Him who came as the Light of the World.

Narrator Two: Yes, Christmas is celebrated in every country where the wonderful news of Jesus' birth is known. In some parts of the world, the Christmas festivities begin four Sundays before December 25 and last until twelve days after Christmas Day. Countries that have long, cold winters find that Christmas comes at a time when there may be much snow on the ground. In other countries the Christmas season comes when the weather is sunny and warm.

Narrator Three: Immigrants who came to make their home in America brought with them customs and traditions of their homelands. Wherever Christmas is celebrated, the singing of Christmas carols is an important part of the festivities. Here are some carolers now.

Song: "Joy to the World." (The children could easily learn the first verse in French.)

(Student enters with a flag of France and mounts it in place. Use a real flag if available or draw one as shown in an encyclopedia on posterboard.)

Narrator Four: France has enriched our heritage of Christmas customs and carols. "The First Noel" is believed to be a French carol even though it was first published in England. The French word *noel* means "a shout of joy" for the newborn King.

Song: "The First Noel."

Narrator Five: There are many Christmas scenes today showing Mary, Joseph, and farm animals gathered around the baby Jesus in a manger. The idea of using the manger scene as a Christmas custom began in France. It was first used by St. Francis of Assisi in the thirteenth century. To teach the people of his parish the story of the first Christmas, he used real animals and people to portray the manger scene.

Song: "Bring a Torch, Jeannette, Isabella."

Narrator Six: Then someone would read the Christmas story: "And they came with haste, and found Mary, and Joseph, and the babe lying in a manger. And when they had seen it, they made known abroad the saying which was told them concerning this child. And all they that heard it wondered at those things which were told them by the shepherds. But Mary kept all these things and pondered them in her heart." (Luke 2:16-19)

Song:	"He Is Born."
Narrator Seven:	Since the time of St. Francis of Assisi, *la crèche* or the manger scene has had an important part in the celebration of Christmas in France. Many French homes display manger scenes with little figures representing the holy family, the wise men, and the animals grouped around the manger. Sometimes candles are lighted on Christmas Eve and kept burning until the twelfth night after Christmas.
Song:	"Angels We Have Heard on High."

(Student enters with a flag of Mexico and mounts it in place.)

Narrator Eight:	Our Mexican neighbors retain many customs from old Spain. One of the loveliest of them is the "posada" or "Resting Place." In Mexico the celebrating begins nine days before Christmas. On that evening, the people gather in the city square or other prominent area.
Narrator Nine:	They form a long procession and walk through the streets, moving from house to house. They usually walk two by two, each carrying a candle. The leaders carry little figures of Mary and Joseph on a litter. One of the men is chosen to knock on doors as the group passes.
Narrator Ten:	Someone inside each home will ask, "Who goes there?" The children in the procession reply, "Mary and Joseph seeking shelter." The voice inside replies, "There is no room." Then the procession moves on.
Song:	"El Nacimiento."
Narrator Eleven:	On the ninth night—Christmas Eve—a door is finally opened to them. One of the men in the candlelight procession is chosen to knock on the door and say, "Listen, I beg you; I am Joseph, and this is my wife, Mary. She has been chosen by God to bear His Son, the King of men!"
Narrator Twelve:	A voice inside responds, "Pardon, good Joseph, for I did not know you. My house is honored by you and the Holy Presence. Great is my joy if you choose to rest here. Enter, I beg you, bless this humble home and bring it happiness."
Narrator Thirteen:	Everyone enters the home to see its elaborately decorated rooms. In one room they see a large bird made from clay or papier mâché hanging from the ceiling. This large bird, called a piñata, has been decorated in bright colors and filled with small gifts and candy. Breaking the piñata is part of the Christmas festivities. The children are blindfolded by turn, then with a heavy stick, they try to hit the swinging piñata. When someone is finally successful in breaking it, the good things inside shower down and the children rush to pick them up.
Song:	"Piñata."

(Students enter with flags of Norway and Sweden and mount them in place.)

Narrator Fourteen:	Norway and Sweden are located in northern Europe and during the Christ-

mas season, their weather is often snowy and cold. But this does not stop the people from celebrating the joy of Christmas. In these countries the carolers that go singing from house to house are often called "star boys" for each one carries a stick or tall pole with a gold paper star fastened to the top. The stars are reminders of the star of the East that the wise men followed to Bethlehem.

Song: "Christmas Eve."

Narrator Fifteen: Christmas festivities begin on St. Lucia's Day in Sweden. On this day, December 13, the children are told the story of Lucia, a Christian girl who was put to death because she refused to give up her faith. According to the legend, St. Lucia came to Sweden during a famine long ago, bringing food for hungry people. She was supposed to have had a white gown and to have worn a crown of light. To honor St. Lucia, each Swedish family chooses a daughter to wear a white gown and a crown made of greenery and lighted candles. Early on the morning of St. Lucia's Day, this daughter awakens the family with her singing as she goes from bedroom to bedroom serving a special breakfast of coffee and buns.

Song: "St. Lucia's Day."

Narrator Sixteen: On the days following December 13, Swedish families make or buy Christmas presents for one another. The gifts are carefully wrapped, sealed with wax, and placed under the Christmas tree. An old custom expects each gift giver to write a special poem that tells the person receiving the gift to perform a simple "forfeit" before he may open the gift.

Narrator Seventeen: At last Christmas Eve arrives. After church services, the families hurry home to a meal that begins with a "dipping ceremony." Each family member dips a piece of bread into a pot of pork broth and eats it. This ceremony honors the winters of famine when families had very little to eat. They then eat a delicious meal which we would call a smorgasbord. After the meal, family members join hands to sing and dance around the Christmas tree.

Song: "Christmas Is Here Again."

Narrator Eighteen: The gifts under the tree are usually given out by the father or an older child who dresses in a red suit and cap. Before anyone can break the wax seal on his gift, he must read the poem from the giver. Paying the "forfeit" that the poem requires is all part of the fun.

Song: "Hejom, Fejom."

Narrator Nineteen: In Scandinavian countries, the good will of the Christmas season is shown by the gifts that family members give to one another. Even the sparrows and other winter birds are remembered and cared for on Christmas Day. The people set out a sheaf of grain on a pole, on a fence or balcony for the birds to enjoy.

Song: "Carole of the Birds."

(Student enters with a flag of Germany and mounts it in place.)

Narrator Twenty: The German people live in a divided country, but the celebration of Christmas has been a part of their custom and tradition for many centuries. This song, "As Each Happy Christmas," is one that originated in Germany.

Song: "As Each Happy Christmas."

Narrator Twenty-one: In Germany the most common symbol of Christmas is the Christmas tree. A traditional legend says that Martin Luther cut a small fir tree in his garden, brought it into his house, and decorated it with candles for his children. He used the tree and the candles to help his children appreciate the beauty of the glistening snow on the trees outdoors. That was the beginning of the custom of indoor Christmas trees as the symbol of lights that honor the Light of the World and of the "ever green" tree.

Narrator Twenty-two: Today when the Christmas tree is decorated and family members gather around it, they may sing, "O Christmas Tree" or another German Christmas carol.

Song: "O Christmas Tree."

Narrator Twenty-three: The hymn, "From Heaven Above," was written in 1534 by Martin Luther for his children and for the observance of Christmas in the Luther home. The tradition was established that a male person dressed like an angel would sing the first seven stanzas and the family would respond and welcome the angel with his great news by singing stanzas eight through fifteen.

Song: "From Heav'n Above to Earth I Come."

(Student enters with a flag of the Netherlands and mounts it in place.)

Narrator Twenty-four: In Holland, December 6 is the most exciting day of the year for boys and girls. This is St. Nicholas or "Sinterklaas" Day. It is named after Nicholas who was elected as the bishop of Myra, a church on the southern coast of Asia Minor in 325 A.D.

Song: "There Comes a Steamboat."

Narrator Twenty-five: St. Nicholas was a good and kind man, and during his lifetime he did much to help people. Since his death, many legends of great things he did have been told and retold.

Narrator Twenty-six: The evening before St. Nicholas Day, the children of Holland get ready for Sinterklaas to visit their homes. They place their shoes by the fireplace and leave a little hay or sugar for Sinterklaas's white horse. The next morning, the hay or sugar is gone and a gift is found in its place.

Narrator Twenty-seven: Santa Claus is the American and English way of saying St. Nicholas. Although the Dutch people celebrate St. Nicholas Day on December 6 as a day quite separate from Christmas on December 25, many people in America have adopted the Dutch customs of St. Nicholas Day as part of their Christmas celebration.

Song: "Up on the Housetop."

Narrator Twenty-eight: Since all the busyness of giving gifts and going to parties takes place early in December on St. Nicholas Day, Christmas in Holland is usually a time of quiet festivity. Many homes have Christmas trees. The Dutch people enjoy listening to and singing Christmas music.

Song: "Stille Nacht."

(Student enters with a flag of Switzerland and mounts it in place.)

Narrator Twenty-nine: Switzerland is often called the country of the Alps. Many Swiss people live in homes on hillsides overlooking villages in the valleys below. Early on Christmas morning, the people arise while it is still dark and go down the mountain pathways, carrying lanterns to light their way as they go to the Christmas worship services.

Narrator Thirty: Church bells sound throughout Switzerland on Christmas to call the people to honor the birthday of the King of kings.

Song: "Ding Dong, Merrily on High."

Narrator Thirty-one: The children of Switzerland, like children in other countries, look forward to receiving Christmas gifts. According to a Swiss legend, the "Christkindel" or Christ child rides in a sleigh drawn by six small reindeer. The Christkindel is represented by a small girl dressed in white wearing a crown of gold. The children never really see her, but they know that she has been there by the presents she brings to them. They listen eagerly for the ringing of a tiny bell that tells she has made a call.

Narrator Thirty-two: The gaiety and happiness of Christmas extend into the week that follows. The grownups do much visiting at their "kaffeklatches." The children dress up in fantastic hats and garments. They use anything from pot lids to cowbells as noisemakers and go from house to house collecting "tributes" of goodies.

Song: "Here We Come A'Wassailing."

(Student enters with a flag of England and mounts it in place.)

Narrator Thirty-three: For many years the people of England have had a custom of singing carols in the streets on Christmas Eve. The song, "Christmas Is Coming," is one of their favorites.

Song: "Christmas Is Coming."

Narrator
Thirty-four: The angels sang the first Christmas carol when they announced the birth of Jesus, our Savior. An angel appeared to some shepherds watching their sheep on a hillside near Bethlehem. He told them that Jesus the Savior was born. After the angel told the shepherds of the Savior's birth, "suddenly there was with the angel a multitude of the heavenly host praising God, and saying, 'Glory to God in the highest, and on earth peace, good will toward men.'" (Luke 2:13, 14)

Narrator
Thirty-five   The English people remind themselves of the joy the shepherds experienced on that first Christmas night long ago by singing carols each Christmas Eve that express feelings of joy and gladness. Here is another one of their favorites.

Song: "We Wish You a Merry Christmas."

Narrator
Thirty-six: The carolers would gather around the front door of a house and sing to those inside. After a few carols had been sung, the people of the home would show their good will and appreciation to the singers by providing them with refreshments. This custom is still carried on, not only in England, but in a number of other European countries as well.

Narrator
Thirty-seven: In England, as in other countries of the world, people begin to prepare for Christmas well before December 25, and the activities of the Christmas season continue for several days afterward. Evergreen boughs are used for decorations. These are usually hung ten days before Christmas and are left up until January 6, the twelfth day after December 25, when they are taken down and burned. According to legend, the fire is supposed to drive out the evil spirits of the past year.

Narrator
Thirty-eight: The ceremony of the "hanging of the greens" has given rise to many legends. For example, in the Middle Ages, it was believed that hanging of mistletoe, yew, or branches of holly and ivy would protect the home from demons which brought cold and darkness in winter.

Song: "The Holly and the Ivy."

Narrator
Thirty-nine: One of the earliest Christmas customs of the people of England was the cutting of the Yule log. All the members of the family would go out to cut the log and gather holly and other evergreens. The Christmas festivities that surrounded the burning of the Yule log in the open fireplace and decorating the home are clearly expressed in the old English carol, "Deck the Halls."

Song: "Deck the Halls."

(Student enters with a flag of the United States and mounts it in place. This flag is to be on the right of the other flags.)

Narrator Forty: Early settlers who came to America generally brought with them the Christmas traditions and customs of their homeland. But there was a group of people that came to America who would never approve of these celebrations. The early Puritans in Massachusetts Bay Colony did not approve of the way the English people celebrated Christmas in their mother country. To keep such "pagan festivity" from gaining foothold in their colony, the Puritans passed the following law in 1659: "Whosoever shall be found observing any such days as Christmas, or the like, either by forbearing of labor, feasting, or in any other way, shall be fined five shillings."

Song: "A Puritan Christmas."

Narrator Forty-one: This law was in effect until 1681. It was not until 1856 that Christmas was recognized as a legal holiday in Massachusetts.

Narrator Forty-two: We have sung some of the Christmas carols that are favorites of people living in other countries of the world. We have told you about some of the Christmas customs they have had in the past. We who live in our country today have a heritage of Christmas customs that have come from many lands. Some of these customs we follow rather closely; others we have blended together; and we have developed new ones of our own as well.

Narrator Forty-three: In this season, Christmas is being celebrated wherever the story of Christ's birth is known. Lights and candles, burning logs and the giving of gifts, the decorations of tree and home all remind us of the joy we have because Christ the Savior was born in Bethlehem's manger. Let us now as Christians join in a spirit of love and praise and conclude our program by singing together a song that is familiar to us all, "O Come, All Ye Faithful."

Song: "O Come, All Ye Faithful."

Adapted from a program written by
Janice Postma and presented at
the Sylvan Christian School,
Grand Rapids

El Nacimiento

Folk Song from Puerto Rico

San Jo-sé y Ma-rí-a a Be-lén lle-ga-ron,

Pi-die-ron po-sa-da y se la ne-ga-ron.

The Piñata

English Words by Nona K. DuffyMexican Folk Song

Bril-liant lan-terns are light-ed, Our friends are in-vit-ed, In cho-rus u-nit-ed, "¡Pi - ña - ta!"

There's no need to re-mind us, With blind-folds they'll bind us, They'll turn and they'll wind us, "¡Pi - ña - ta!"

Ay, que bue - na, Ay, que bue - na, Ay, que bue - na, que bue - na, que bue - na.

All the chil-dren will scram-ble for can-dy,
All the chil-dren will grab for a cook-y

All the chil-dren will scram-ble and shout;
And the oth-er good things that spill out.

St. Lucia's Day

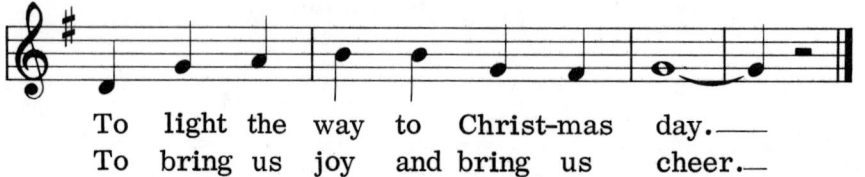

English Words by Alice Firgau
Swedish Carol

Joyfully

1. Wake up, Lucia comes today.
2. Wake up, Lucia greets us here.

Oh, be glad! Lucia comes in bright array
Lucia comes again this year

To light the way to Christmas day.
To bring us joy and bring us cheer.

3. She enters with the morning light.
   Oh, be glad!
   Her happy face, 'neath candles bright,
   Dispels the darkness of the night.

4. This day our hearts are filled with love.
   Oh, be glad!
   Lucia tells of God's great love
   And of His gift from heav'n above.

Christmas Is Here Again

English Translation by Coleman and Jörgensen

Swedish Folk Song

Descant:
Ding - dong! Ding - dong! Ding - dong, ding - dong!
Ding - dong! Ding - dong! Ding - dong! Ding - dong!

Melody:
Christ-mas is here a - gain, Oh, Christ-mas is here a - gain, Our hol - i - days will last till Eas - ter. Then it is Eas - ter - time, Oh, then it is Eas - ter - time, And Eas - ter joy will last till Christ - mas.

Words copyright, 1934, 1961, G. Schirmer, Inc. Reprinted by permission.

Hejom, Fejom

English Words by Ruth Tooze
Swedish Folk Song

1. Watch when you o-pen this gift so gay,
2. Shut your eyes tight when you o-pen this,

He - jom, fe - jom, fal - li - ral - li - ra.

For some-thing may jump out, then you can play,
To find a sur-prise that you must not miss.

He - jom, fe - jom, fal - li - ral - li - ra.

3. Hop on one foot and untie the string.
   Then you'll make us laugh as you dance and sing.

4. Mother, you must feed the birds today.
   Before you can open the wrappings gay.

O Christmas Tree

German Folk Carol

O Christ-mas tree, O Christ-mas tree, with branch-es ev - er glow - ing,

In sum-mer, green and fair you grow,

In win - ter dressed in pur - est snow.

O Christ - mas tree, O Christ - mas tree,

With branch - es ev - er glow - ing.

There Comes a Steamboat

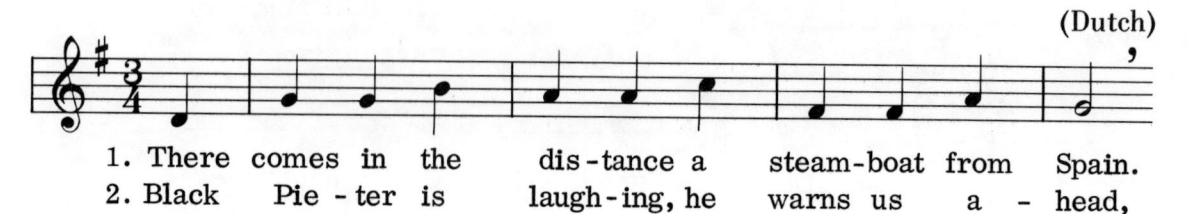

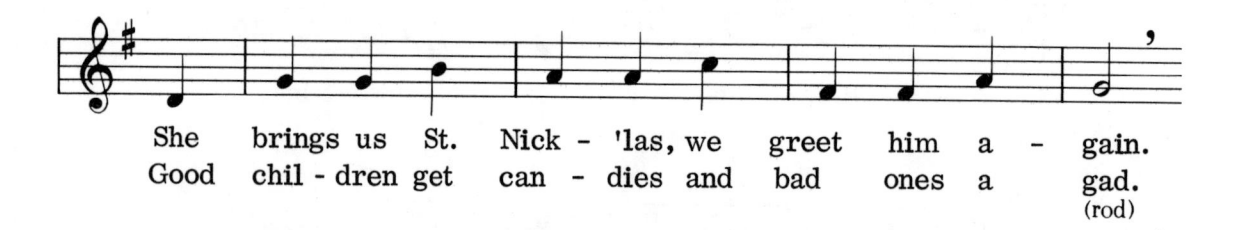

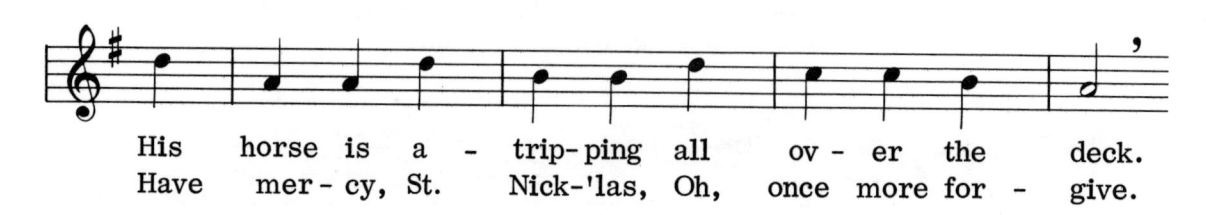

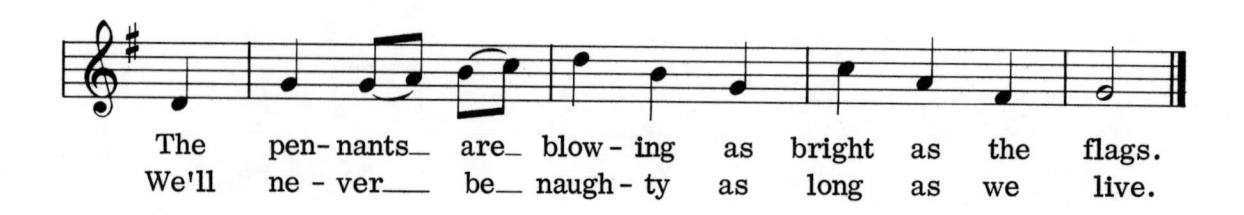

(Dutch)

1. There comes in the dis-tance a steam-boat from Spain.
2. Black Pie-ter is laugh-ing, he warns us a-head,

She brings us St. Nick-'las, we greet him a-gain.
Good chil-dren get can-dies and bad ones a gad.
(rod)

His horse is a-trip-ping all ov-er the deck.
Have mer-cy, St. Nick-'las, Oh, once more for-give.

The pen-nants are blow-ing as bright as the flags.
We'll ne-ver be naugh-ty as long as we live.

Up on the Housetop

Words and music by Benjamin T. Hanby

1. Up on the house-top the rein-deer pause,
Out jumps good old San-ta Claus;
Down through the chim-ney with lots of toys,
All for the lit-tle ones' Christ-mas joys.

Refrain
Ho, ho, ho, Who would-n't go!
Ho, ho, ho, Who would-n't go!
Up on the house-top, click, click, click,
Down through the chim-ney with good Saint Nick.

2. First comes the stocking of little Nell;
   Oh, dear Santa, fill it well.
   Give her a dolly that laughs and cries,
   One that can open and shut its eyes.

3. Look in the stocking of little Bill;
   Oh, just see what a glorious fill!
   Here is a hammer, and lots of tacks,
   Whistle and ball and a whip that cracks.

Ding, Dong, Merrily on High

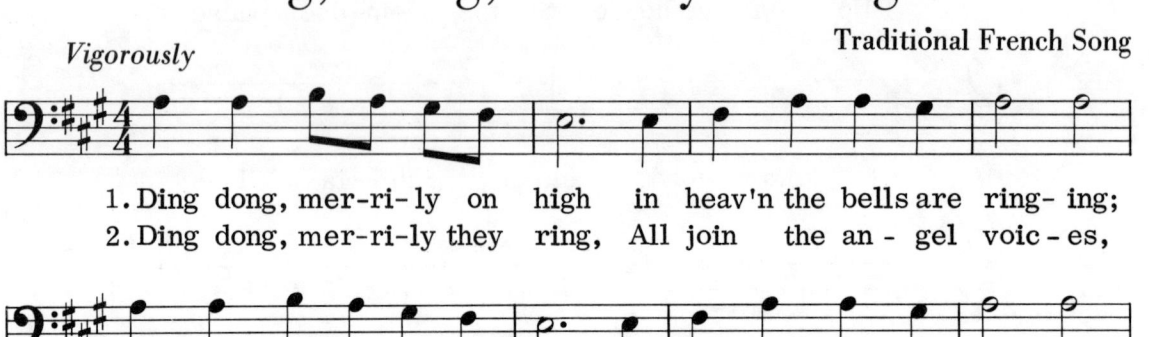

Traditional French Song

Vigorously

1. Ding dong, mer-ri-ly on high in heav'n the bells are ring-ing;
2. Ding dong, mer-ri-ly they ring, All join the an-gel voic-es,

Ding dong, ver-i-ly the sky is riv'n with an-gel sing-ing.
Ding dong, mer-ri-ly they sing, Hear how the world re-joic-es.

Glo - - - ri - a, glo -
Glo - - - ri - a, glo -
Glo - - - ri - a, glo -

ri - a, Ho - san - na in ex - cel - sis.
ri - a, Ho - san - na in ex - cel - sis.
ri - a, Ho - san - na in ex - cel - sis.

Christmas Is Coming

Author Unknown
English Tune

1. Christ - mas is com - ing! The goose is get - ting fat!
Please to put a pen - ny in an old man's hat,
Please to put a pen - ny in an old man's hat.

2. If you've no pen - ny, A ha' - pen - ny will do,
If you have no ha' - pen - ny, Then God bless you,
If you have no ha' - pen - ny, Then God bless you.

This carol may be sung as a round.

A Puritan Christmas

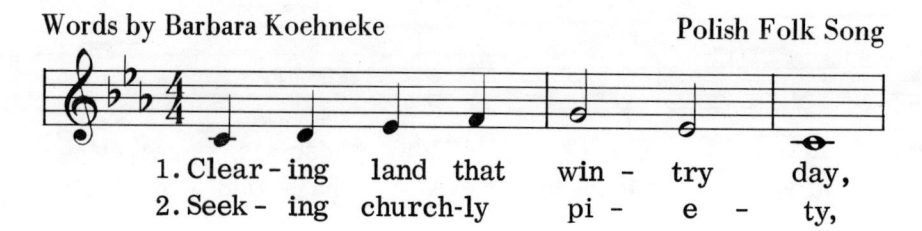

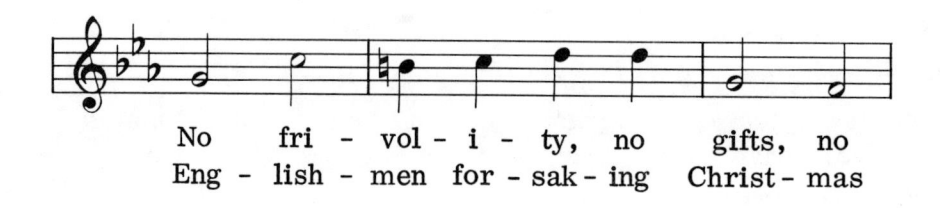

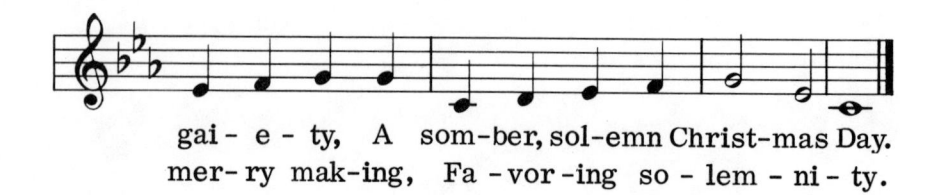

Words by Barbara Koehneke

Polish Folk Song

1. Clear-ing land that win-try day,
Strug-gling for a place to stay,
No fri-vol-i-ty, no gifts, no gai-e-ty,
A som-ber, sol-emn Christ-mas Day.

2. Seek-ing church-ly pi-e-ty,
They for-bade fes-tiv-i-ty.
Eng-lish-men for-sak-ing Christ-mas mer-ry mak-ing,
Fa-vor-ing so-lem-ni-ty.

A NIGHT TO REMEMBER

Narrator: Christmas Day will soon be here. Most of us make plans for celebrating the Christmas season long before it comes. No other time of the year fills us with such a glow of happiness. We all engage in festivities, merrymaking, and glad tidings. After all, it's Christmas time! Notes and words echo throughout the world proclaiming the spirit of the season. But what do we hear? Listen to the familiar sounds which captivate the minds of young and old. **It's Christmas!**

(Play short selections from tunes like "Silver Bells," "Rudolph the Red-nosed Reindeer," "Jingle Bells," and "I'm Dreaming of a White Christmas." These can be pretaped and played in the background while the narrator continues.)

Narrator: What does all this mean? Are we attempting to cover up the true meaning of Christmas? Surely the music is lilting and expresses a feeling of warmth and happiness, but after the season is over people will again feel the burdens of another year awaiting them. What lasting impression has Christmas really made? It is our desire and prayer that through our presentation this evening the true meaning of Christmas will be portrayed and that our hearts will be filled with love in reponse to God's wonderful gift of love—the Lord Jesus Christ.

(Family enters from rear of sanctuary or auditorium. The father is looking glum, and follows along reluctantly.)

Father: Do I really have to go to this program? I'll be missing my football game, and besides, I have other things I'd rather do.

Joey: Please, Dad, we've been learning such great songs and the story we're going to tell—well, it's the greatest story ever told! Please, Dad.

Mother: You're coming with us, like it or not! At least you can show some interest in your son's church school.

Father: Okay, but don't bother me anymore. I'll go this time, but never again!

(Family takes position in front seats.)

Speech Choir: The voice of him that crieth in the wilderness,
Prepare ye the way of the Lord,
   make straight in the desert a highway
   for our God.
Every valley shall be exalted, and every
   mountain and hill shall be made low:
And the crooked shall be made straight, and
   the rough places plain:
And the glory of the Lord shall be revealed,
   and all flesh shall see it together:
For the mouth of the Lord hath spoken it.

Narrator: And so it was prophesied in the Old Testament that someday God would fulfill His promise to send His Son, the Savior of the world. This promise

	would soon be fulfilled—an event to which every God-fearing Israelite was looking forward.
Processional:	"Come, Thou Long-expected Jesus"
	(A colorful overhead of the Mediterranean world, including Judea, could be projected on the screen during the following narration.)
Narrator:	In those days Rome ruled the world. Rome—the great city of the West, the city built on the greatness of the Greeks, an empire built on structures and ideas which boggle the human mind. Rome—whose power was felt all over the Mediterranean world. With her armies, known as legions, she held captive the countries of her empire. One such country was Palestine, which included the province of Judea. The setting of the stage for things to come didn't *just happen by chance.* No, indeed! God used this pagan, humanistic culture to carry out His eternal plan in the fullness of time. In the province of Judea a decree was heard that led to confusion in the little town of Bethlehem.

Speech Choir:	But thou, Bethlehem Ephratah, though thou
	    be little among the thousands of Judah,
	Yet out of thee shall he come forth unto me
	    that is to be ruler in Israel;
	Whose goings forth have been from of old,
	    from everlasting.

	(A Roman soldier appears on stage with a scroll in his hands. He reads from the scroll.)
Soldier:	Hear ye! Hear ye! I, Caesar Augustus, most noble of all Romans, do make this proclamation to all people in the Roman Empire: Every person in my dominion must be enrolled and taxed. This decree goes out to north Africa, Turkey, Egypt, and to all of Palestine. Each one must be enrolled in the city or town of his birth. All governors and deputies must see that this edict is strictly enforced.
Speech Choir:	And it came to pass in those days, that there went out a decree from Caesar Augustus, that all the world should be taxed. And this taxing was first made when Cyrenius was governor of Syria. And all went to be taxed, every one to his own city. And Joseph also went up from Galilee, out of the city of Nazareth, into Judea, unto the city of David, which is called *Bethlehem;* because he was of the house and lineage of David: to be taxed with Mary his espoused wife, being great with child.
	(A clashing of cymbals is heard off-stage. Soldiers enter the scene and march to their places. They stand at attention during the singing of the next song.)
Children's Choir:	"Once in Royal David's City" or "O Little Town of Bethlehem"
	(Enter pilgrims looking for a place to stay the night. Joseph steps forward and approaches one of the soldiers.)
Joseph:	Excuse me, sir, but do you know of a place where my wife and I can spend the night?

Soldier:	*(rudely)* I'm too busy to be bothered with such things. Be on your way.

(Some of the pilgrims go into an inn, but a family of four is turned away by the innkeepers. Joseph meets the pilgrims who were turned away.)

Joseph:	*(speaking to one of the pilgrims)* Sir, can you please help me? My wife and I desperately need a place to stay tonight. Do you know of such a place?
Pilgrim:	My family was just turned away from the inn, but there may be room for only two of you.

(Joseph nods his thanks; the family of four exits. Joseph walks to the inn. The innkeeper meets him at the door.)

Innkeeper:	If it's shelter you need, there's no room here.
Joseph:	*(protesting)* But sir, we've come a long way and my wife is going to have her baby very soon, perhaps tonight. Is there no room even for us?
Innkeeper:	I'm sorry, we're full.

(Joseph shakes his head sadly and turns to walk away.)

Innkeeper:	Wait! There is a place in my stable, although you may not want to stay there. The Romans don't think it's good enough for their horses!
Joseph:	Thank you; we will stay there tonight. Mary cannot travel any farther.

(Everyone exits.)

Speech Choir:	And so it was, that, while they were there, the days were accomplished that she should be delivered. And she brought forth her firstborn son, and wrapped him in swaddling clothes, and laid him in a manger; because there was no room for them in the inn.
Children's Choir:	"Away in a Manger"
Narrator:	And the prophecies of the Old Testament were fulfilled.
First Speaker:	Behold the days come, saith the Lord, that I will raise unto David a righteous Branch, and a King shall reign and prosper, and shall execute judgment and justice in the earth.
Second Speaker:	But unto you that fear my name shall the Sun of righteousness arise with healing in his wings.
Third Speaker:	For unto us a child is born, unto us a son is given: and the government shall be upon his shoulder:
All Speakers:	And his name shall be called Wonderful, Counselor, the mighty God, the everlasting Father, the Prince of Peace.
Third Speaker:	Of the increase of his government and peace there shall be no end, upon the throne of David, and upon his kingdom, to order it, and to establish it with judgment and justice from henceforth even for ever. The zeal of the Lord of hosts will perform this.

(Stage is set with the manger scene: Mary, Joseph, and the Baby.)

Choir: "Coventry Carol" or "Oh, Leave Your Sheep"

(During the singing of the preceding carol, several shepherds enter and gather around the manger, kneeling in worship.)

Choir: "What Child Is This," "From Heaven Above to Earth I Come," and "What Can I Give Him"

Narrator: The shepherds brought their humble praises to the Christ child. They did not have gold and jewels to offer Him, but they gave Him their love and devotion. Later the wise men came from the east, following the star and bringing rich gifts. These Magi were themselves kings, but they recognized Jesus as the King of kings and brought Him their worship. Listen as they tell their story.

(Three boys enter, dressed in colorful robes and holding gifts in their hands. They stand center stage.)

Choir: "We Three Kings of Orient Are"

(At stanza two, one wise man steps forward with his gift of gold; at stanza three, the second one with his gift of frankincense; and at stanza four, the third one with his gift of myrrh. All join in singing stanza five. After the song all the program participants join the three kings on the platform.)

Hymn: "Joy to the World."

Narrator: This was the story of long ago when Christ was born. We are glad you came to share the true meaning of Christmas with us.

(Music plays as the program participants leave the stage and return to their seats in the auditorium. The stage is set with a family scene. It is Christmas Eve. The family leave their front row seats and come on stage.)

Mother: Hurry, children, let's quickly finish decorating the tree. It's almost time to open the presents. Look, here's one from Uncle Bert; here's one from Dad to—let's see—it says, "Joey"!

Joey: That's for me! I can't wait to open it!

Mother: Look, here is one for Dad from Cindy.

Dad: *(Taking Cindy on his lap)* You bought a present for your Dad. Thank you, Cindy. I'm sure I will like it if you picked it out.

Mother: Okay, Dad. I think we are ready to light the tree.

Children: How pretty!

Dad: Before we open our gifts, I wonder if we can each give one reason why presents are given at Christmas. You see, a week ago I did not want to go to your program, Joey. But tonight I am so happy that I did go—I learned the true meaning of Christmas that night. It is a celebration of God's giving us His Son, the Lord Jesus Christ. This is the gift God gave us so willingly and freely that all we must do is believe in Him and accept His gift to us. Sharing the good news of salvation is also a part of celebrating Christmas. Others must be able to see that our lives are different because of the life of the Lord Jesus Christ. Let's name some of God's wonderful gifts to us which we can share with others.

Children: Kindness
Love
Patience
Humility
Understanding
Happiness

Mother: It is so easy to forget the gift of happiness. As Christians we must be happy in work or play. There is never a reason for a Christian to wear a long, grumpy face. How can we expect others to believe the good news of the gospel if we do not show joy?

Child: Listen, I believe I hear some carolers.

(Carolers are heard off-stage. Dad goes to the door and invites them in.)

One Caroler: We are here to bring your family the good news of Christmas. Would you like to join us as we go to the rest of the neighborhood and sing? It's cold out, but it's lots of fun.

Children: Please, Dad! Let's go!

Dad: It's all right with me. This is the greatest Christmas I have ever had. First I found out what Christmas is all about at your program, and now I'm going to learn about the happiness of sharing the good news of God's gift to us.

(The family and carolers walk to the front of the stage and the entire audience joins in singing carols.)

Closing Prayer

Recessional

Adapted from a program written by
Sue Hamstra, Joyce Katje,
Sue Terborg, Leanne Van Dyk,
and Ivan W. Van Essen

HE IS ALTOGETHER LOVELY

(This program is designed for organ, speech choir, and eight individual speakers. The organ music forms the background and fades out as the speaking parts begin. The speech choir should be inconspicuously positioned but in a place from which their voices are distinctly heard.)

Organ: "Silent Night," "O Come, All Ye Faithful," "Joy to the World," or any other familiar Christmas carols.

(While the organ is still playing the scientist enters and takes a position center stage.)

Scientist: I am the wisdom of the world. I am a scientist. I have diplomas, degrees, honors—I have wealth. I am respected. My mind is sharp: I can solve the mysteries of the universe; I know the stars; I measure the skies; I fathom the depth of the seas. But *(gesturing)* I cannot understand all this fuss about Christmas!

Speech Choir: For unto us a child is born, unto us a son is given:
And the government shall be upon his shoulder:
And his name shall be called **Wonderful,**
    Counselor, The mighty God,
The everlasting Father,
The Prince of Peace.

(Organ plays softly, "For All the Saints" or "I Am a Stranger Here." Christian enters carrying her Bible and slowly walks across the platform.)

Scientist: Wait! Stop a moment! Who are you? Where are you going? Why do you have that book with you?

Christian: I'm a Christian. I am a stranger and a pilgrim here. This book shows me the way to the city which God has prepared for all those who believe in His Son the Lord Jesus Christ, whose birthday we are celebrating today.

Scientist: But why are you dressed in white?

Christian: To show that my sins have been washed away in the blood of the Lamb who was sacrificed on the cross for me. I am dressed in the robe of righteousness of my Lord and Savior, Jesus Christ.

Speech Choir: I will greatly rejoice in the Lord,
My soul shall be joyful in my God;
For he hath clothed me with the garments of salvation,
He hath covered me with the **robe of righteousness,**
As a bridegroom decketh himself with ornaments,
    and as a bride adorneth herself with her jewels.

Scientist: These things sound strange to me. You appear to be poor and without worldly knowledge and yet you seem to be happy!

Christian: Dear scientist, you do not yet understand that the wisdom of this world is foolishness with God.

Speech Choir: But God hath chosen the foolish things of the world to confound the wise;

and God hath chosen the weak things of the world to confound the things which are mighty; And base things of the world, and things which are despised, hath God chosen, yea, and things which are not, to bring to nought things that are: that no flesh should glory in his presence.

Christian: God has made the way of salvation so clear that even children and the simple-minded can understand. It is the way of love which God showed us when He sent His only Son to be our Savior.

Speech Choir: Though I speak with the tongues of men and of angels, and have not love,
I am become as sounding brass, or a tinkling cymbal.

And though I have the gift of prophecy, and understand all mysteries, and all knowledge; and though I have all faith, so that I could remove mountains, and have not love,
I am nothing.

And though I bestow all my goods to feed the poor, and though I give my body to be burned, and have not love,
It profiteth me nothing....

Love never faileth: but whether there be prophecies, they shall fail; whether there be tongues, they shall cease; whether there be knowledge, it shall vanish away.

(As the organ begins to play "Break Thou the Bread of Life" or "Come, for the Feast is Spread," the scientist and Christian move to one side of the stage. The baker enters carrying a loaf of bread. Organ music fades as baker speaks.)

Baker: I am a baker. Each day thousands of loaves of bread leave my shop to feed hungry people. Yet the people soon become hungry again and they come to buy more bread. Though they eat the finest of my bread they are never completely satisfied and would die if they didn't eat regularly. But Jesus said, "I am the bread of life: he that cometh to me shall never hunger; and he that believeth on me shall never thirst."

Speech Choir: The Lord Jesus the night in which he was betrayed took bread: And when he had given thanks, he broke it, and said:

Solo Voice: Take, eat: this is my body, which is broken for you: this do in remembrance of me.

Speech Choir: After the same manner also he took the cup, when he had supped, saying,

Solo Voice: This cup is the new testament in my blood: this do ye, as oft as ye drink it, in remembrance of me.

Speech Choir: For as often as ye eat this bread, and drink this cup, ye do show the Lord's death till he comes.

(While the organ plays "The Lord's My Shepherd" the baker stands back and the shepherd enters and moves to center stage. Organ fades as shepherd speaks.)

Shepherd: I am a shepherd. I love my sheep. I walk many weary miles to bring back my wandering and lost sheep. But I myself am a sheep in the fold of Jesus. Jesus is the Good Shepherd who laid down His life for His sheep. Today is

Christmas, His birthday. Jesus, my Shepherd, said, "My sheep hear my voice, and I know them, and they follow me: And I give unto them eternal life; and they shall never perish, neither shall any man pluck them out of my hand.

Speech Choir: The Lord is my shepherd;
I shall not want.
He maketh me to lie down in green pastures:
He leadeth me beside the still waters.
He restoreth my soul:
He leadeth me in the paths of righteousness
for his name's sake.

Yea, though I walk through
the valley of the shadow of death,
I will fear no evil:
for thou art with me;
Thy rod and thy staff they comfort me.

Thou preparest a table before me in the
presence of mine enemies:
Thou anointest my head with oil;
My cup runneth over.

Surely goodness and mercy shall follow me
all the days of my life:
And I will dwell in the house of the Lord forever.

(Organ plays, "There Is a Fountain Filled with Blood" or "Just As I Am, Without One Plea." The water carrier enters carrying a pail of water.)

Water Carrier: I am only a water carrier. But I carry a necessity of life. How quickly we would all perish without water! How refreshing is a cool drink of water when we are hot and tired! Yet though we drink of this water several times a day we become thirsty again. But Jesus offers us living water. He said, "Whosoever drinketh of the water that I shall give him shall never thirst; but the water that I shall give him shall be in him a well of water springing up into everlasting life."

Speech Choir: Ho, every one that thirsteth,
Come to the water, and he that hath no money;
   come ye, buy, and eat;
Yea, come, buy wine and milk **without** money
   and **without** price.

And the Spirit and the bride say, **Come.**
And let him that heareth say, **Come.**
And let him that is athirst come.
And whosoever will,
   let him take the water of life **freely.**

(Organ plays, "Jesus, Priceless Treasure." As the water carrier steps back, a rich man enters wearing expensive-looking clothes and jewels.)

Rich Man: I am rich. I have money, houses, lands. I have much more of everything than I need in my lifetime. However, if I did not have Jesus I would still be poor. Jesus said, "For what is a man profited, if he shall gain the whole world, and lose his own soul?"

(Organ plays, "Beautiful Savior" or "Fairest Lord Jesus." As the rich man steps aside, a man with some gardening tools enters.)

Gardener: My business is to grow flowers. Roses are my specialty. My roses are famous all over the world. But their beauty is only a faint reflection of the beauty of my Savior. He is the Rose of Sharon, the Lily of the Valley.

Speech Choir: Give unto the Lord the glory due unto his name;
Worship the Lord in the beauty of holiness.

Honor and majesty are before him:
Strength and beauty are in his sanctuary. . . .

O worship the Lord in beauty of holiness:
Fear before him, all the earth. . . .

Let the heavens rejoice, and let the earth be glad;
Let the sea roar and the fullness thereof.
Let the field be joyful,
   and all that is therein:
     then shall all the trees of the wood
     rejoice before the Lord:

For he cometh,
For he cometh to judge the earth:
He shall judge the world with righteousness,
And the people with his truth.

(The organ continues to play, "Beautiful Savior" or "Fairest Lord Jesus" as the gardener stands aside and Truth enters dressed in white and carrying a Bible.)

Truth: I am Truth *(raising the Bible)*. I have the Word of truth which God gave to the world. Jesus said to those who believe, "If ye continue in my word, then are ye my disciples indeed; and ye shall know the truth, and the truth shall make you free."

Scientist: *(longingly)* O, Truth, I have sought you all of my life! Tell me *(gesturing toward all those on stage)*, have all these spoken the truth? Is Jesus really all they say?

Truth: Yes, dear scientist. They have spoken the Word of the Lord which stands forever. God is not a man that He should lie. His words make the simple wise. They give light to those in darkness. God's Word never fails!

Scientist: If what you say is true, I must bid farewell to worldly wisdom! I accept the truth of God's Word and join all those who are on their way to the city which God has prepared for those who believe in His Son, the Lord Jesus Christ.

(As the organ begins to play softly, "By the Sea of Crystal," the scientist kneels with hands raised. All participants form a group around him and everyone, including the audience, joins in singing, "By the Sea of Crystal." [Music is on page 23]

Adapted from a play written by
J. W. F. Uitvlugt

THE PATHWAY OF PROMISE

The stage for this program can be set with the "versatile Christmas tree" (see page 100) at one side so that it can be spotlighted at appropriate times. As each participant enters, the symbol (see pages 101-107) which he represents will be attached to the tree. Toward the end of the program, the foliage and symbols will be removed with only the cross remaining. The stage background can be a mural depicting a road leading from the Garden of Eden to Calvary. Several weeks before the program is to be given, the work of making the pictures for it could be assigned to various groups of children. Their art work can be an important part of preparing them for the presentation of the program. One class could make pictures depicting the Garden of Eden and the patriarchs; another class, pictures of the prophets; another group, scenes of Bethlehem and Calvary. All of these pictures would then be placed on the mural to complete the "Pathway of Promise" as it is unfolded in the program.

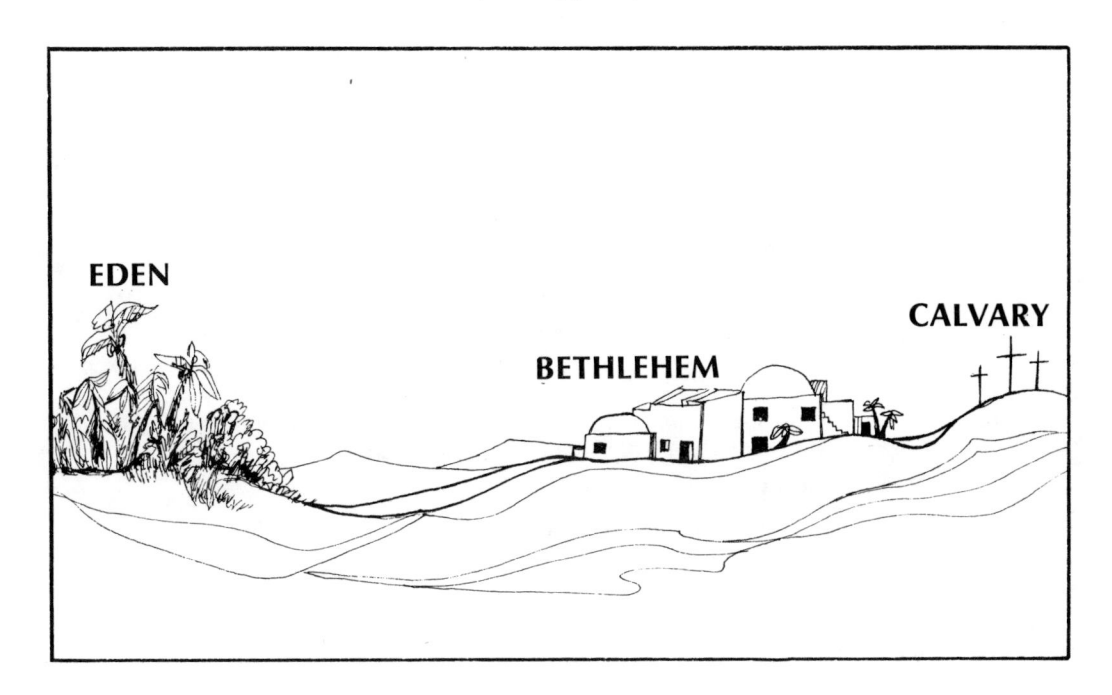

Processional:	"O Come, All Ye Faithful"
Leader:	All of God's faithful ones belong to a vast throng of travelers who are journeying toward the city of eternal day which has been promised to them by God. Tonight, we would like to take you back in time. Follow with us the pathway of promise from the Garden of Eden to Bethlehem and to Calvary.
Choir:	"Watchman, Tell Us of the Night"

Watchman, tell us of the night,
What its signs of promise are.
Traveler, o'er yon mountain's height,
See that glory-beaming star.
Watchman, does its beauteous ray
Aught of joy or hope foretell?
Traveler, yes; it brings the day,
Promised day of Israel.

95

Watchman, tell us of the night,
Higher yet that star ascends.
Traveler, blessedness and light,
Peace and truth its course portends.
Watchman, will its beams alone
Gild the spot that gave them birth?
Traveler, ages are its own;
See, it bursts o'er all the earth.

Watchman, tell us of the night,
For the morning seems to dawn.
Traveler, darkness takes its flight,
Doubt and terror are withdrawn.
Watchman, let thy wanderings cease;
Hie thee to thy quiet home.
Traveler, lo, the Prince of Peace,
Lo, the Son of God is come.

Cara

Eve: My name is Eve. The promise of a Savior was first given to Adam and me in the Garden of Eden. God told Satan that he would eventually be conquered and destroyed by one of our descendants. God said:

> I will put enmity between thee and the woman, and between thy seed and her seed; it shall bruise thy head, and thou shalt bruise his heel. (GEN. 3:15)

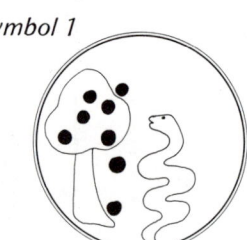

Symbol 1

Danny

Abraham: My name is Abraham. Nearly twenty-five years before Sarah and I had a son, God told me the Savior would be born of my lineage. He said:

> I will make of thee a great nation, and I will bless thee, and make thy name great; and thou shalt be a blessing: And I will bless them that bless thee, and curse him that curseth thee: and in thee shall all families of the earth be blessed. (GEN. 12:2,3)

Symbol 2

Max

Judah: My name is Judah. Before my father Jacob died, he prophesied that my family had been chosen for the royal line of the Savior-King. He said:

> The sceptre shall not depart from Judah, nor a lawgiver from between his feet, until Shiloh come; and unto him shall the gathering of the people be. (GEN. 49:10)

Symbol 3

Tyson

Moses: My name is Moses. God gave us His perfect law to teach us how to live, but we continually went astray from the pathway of promise. God always forgave our sins and promised us salvation. He told us that the Savior would be a prophet-teacher. He said:

> I will raise them up a Prophet from among their brethren, like unto thee, and I will put my words in his mouth; and he shall speak unto them all that I shall command him. (DEUT. 18:18)

Symbol 4

Christine

David: My name is David. When Samuel came to my father's house to anoint a king in the place of Saul, he was sure that my oldest brother, Eliab, was the chosen one because he was so tall and handsome. But God said to Samuel, "The Lord seeth not as

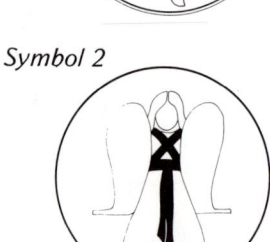

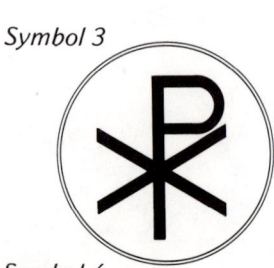

Symbol 5

man seeth; for man looketh on the outward appearance, but the Lord looketh on the heart." God chose me—a shepherd boy—not only to be the king of Israel but also to be the ancestor of our Savior, the Good Shepherd. (I Sam. 16:7)

Choir: "O Come, O Come, Emmanuel" ok

Leader: God's chosen people strayed far from the pathway of promise. Many prophets were sent to warn them of their coming exile and to repeat God's unfailing promises to those who were looking for the Messiah. Listen to some of these voices from the past.

Denny

Isaiah: For unto us a child is born, unto us a son is given: and the government shall be upon his shoulder: and his name shall be called Wonderful, Counselor, The mighty God, The everlasting Father, The Prince of Peace. Of the increase of his government and peace there shall be no end, upon the throne of David, and upon his kingdom, to order it, and to establish it with judgment and with justice from henceforth even for ever. *(Isaiah 9:6, 7)* — Symbol 6

Amy

Jeremiah: Behold, the days come, saith the Lord, that I will make a new covenant with the house of Israel, and with the house of Judah: not according to the covenant that I made with their fathers in the day that I took them by the hand to bring them out of the land of Egypt;... But this shall be the covenant that I will make... I will put my law in their inward parts, and write it in their hearts; and will be their God, and they shall be my people. *(Jeremiah 31:31-33)* — Symbol 7

Bobby

Ezekiel: I will save my flock, and they shall no more be a prey.... And I will set up one shepherd over them, and he shall feed them, even my servant David; he shall feed them, and he shall be their shepherd. And I the Lord will be their God, and my servant David a prince among them. *(Ezekiel 34:22-24)* — Symbol 8

Jenny

Daniel: I saw in the night visions, and, behold, one like the Son of man came with the clouds of heaven, and came to the Ancient of days, and they brought him near before him. And there was given him dominion, and glory, and a kingdom, that all people, nations, and languages, should serve him: his dominion is an everlasting dominion, which shall not pass away, and his kingdom that which shall not be destroyed. *(Daniel 7:13, 14)* — Symbol 9

Danny

Micah: But thou, Bethlehem Ephratah, though thou be little among the thousands of Judah, yet out of thee shall he come forth unto me that is to be ruler in Israel; whose goings forth have been of old, from everlasting. *(Micah 5:2)* — Symbol 10

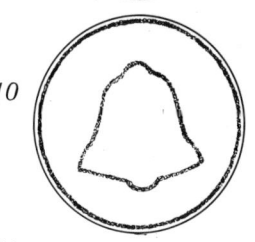

Christine

Zechariah: Rejoice greatly, O daughter of Zion; shout, O daughter of Jerusalem: behold, thy King cometh unto thee: he is just, and having salvation; lowly and riding upon an ass, and upon a colt the foal of an ass. *(Zechariah 9:9)* — Symbol 11

Choir: ~~"Come, Thou Long-expected Jesus"~~

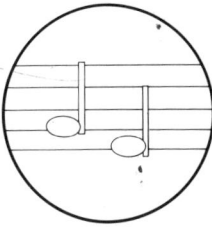

"All Glory, Laud, and Honor" ~~struck through~~
"Hark! the Herald Angels Sing" *sing*

Leader: After the last Old Testament prophet had spoken, God's people waited yet another four hundred years for the Messiah to come. In the fullness of time God's never-failing promises were fulfilled. The pathway of promise now leads us to Bethlehem.

Choir: "O Little Town of Bethlehem" *ok*

Leader: And it came to pass in those days, that there went out a decree from Caesar Augustus, that all the world should be taxed. . . . And all went to be taxed, every one into his own city. And Joseph also went up from Galilee, into Judea, unto the city of David, which is called Bethlehem; . . . to be taxed with Mary his espoused wife, being great with child. And so it was, that, while they were there, the days were accomplished that she should be delivered. And she brought forth her firstborn son, and wrapped him in swaddling clothes, and laid him in a manger; because there was no room for them in the inn. *(Luke 2:1-7)*

Choir: "Angels, from the Realms of Glory" — *Sing*
~~"Angels We Have Heard on High"~~

Leader: It is fitting that shepherds should have been the first to hear the good news of the Savior's birth. Listen as they tell their story.

First Shepherd: [*Max*] It was night and we were watching over our sheep in the fields *Symbol 12* near Bethlehem. Suddenly a great light shone on us: it was an angel of the Lord.

Second Shepherd: [*Tyson*] We were afraid, but the angel said,
"Fear not: for, behold, I bring you good tidings of great joy, which shall be to all people. For unto you is born this day in the city of David a Savior, which is Christ the Lord. And this shall be a sign unto you; Ye shall find the babe wrapped in swaddling clothes, lying in a manger." *(Luke 2: 10-12)*

Third Shepherd: [*Danny*] Suddenly there appeared a host of angels praising God and saying, "Glory to God in the highest, and on earth peace, good will toward men."

Fourth Shepherd: [*Amy*] After the angels returned to heaven we left our sheep and went immediately to Bethlehem to see this wonderful Child who the angels told us was born. We found Mary and Joseph and the Babe lying in a manger. We told Mary and Joseph about the angels' message. Then we went out and told everyone we met about this wonderful event.

Choir: "We Three Kings of Orient Are" — *Boys? ask them*

Leader: Travelers from the east were guided to Bethlehem by a star. They came with rich gifts for the Child-King and worshiped Him.

First Wise Man: [*Bobby*] We saw His star in the east and are come to worship Him. I *Symbol 13* offer Him my gift of gold.

Cara

Second Wise Man: We traveled a long way but have found Him who is born to be King of kings. I give to Him my gift of myrrh.

Jenny

Third Wise Man: We found this wonderful Babe, not in a palace, but in a lowly dwelling. My gift is the frankincense from the forest.

Choir: ~~"Lo, How a Rose" or "All My Heart This Night Rejoices"~~ *Kids — two songs*

~~Remove symbols and foliage.~~

Leader: All promises were fulfilled in Christ, beginning with His birth at Bethlehem where He emptied Himself of His glory and power. He lived a sinless life and thus fulfilled God's perfect law for us and finally made the supreme sacrifice for our sins at Calvary.

~~**Choir:**~~ ~~"Ah, Dearest Jesus" or "What Wondrous Love"~~

Leader: All travelers on the pathway of promise must not only worship the Babe of Bethlehem but must also kneel in repentance at Calvary. Christ died for sin, *once for all*. After leaving our burden of sin at the cross, we can continue our journey to the city of eternal day. Won't you join us on the pathway of promise ~~tonight?~~ *today?*

Choir: ~~"Alleluia! Sing to Jesus" or "Hark! Ten Thousand Harps and Voices"~~

#174 As with Gladness Men of Old

99

A VERSATILE CHRISTMAS TREE

The trunk and branches which form the cross are constructed from plywood and laminated with brown burlap.

The foliage is cut from a sheet of styrofoam about one inch thick. It is laminated with green burlap with an overlay of brown for the branches. Two hooks are inserted in the back of the tree so it can be hung on the cross and easily removed at the appropriate moment in the program.

The various symbols are made from a circular styrofoam base about 1 inch thick. These can be cut with a one-pound coffee can or any other can with a sharp edge. The symbols are decorated with tinsel, glitter, felt, tin foil and other bright materials. Insert hat pins through the completed symbols so they can be easily attached to the tree.

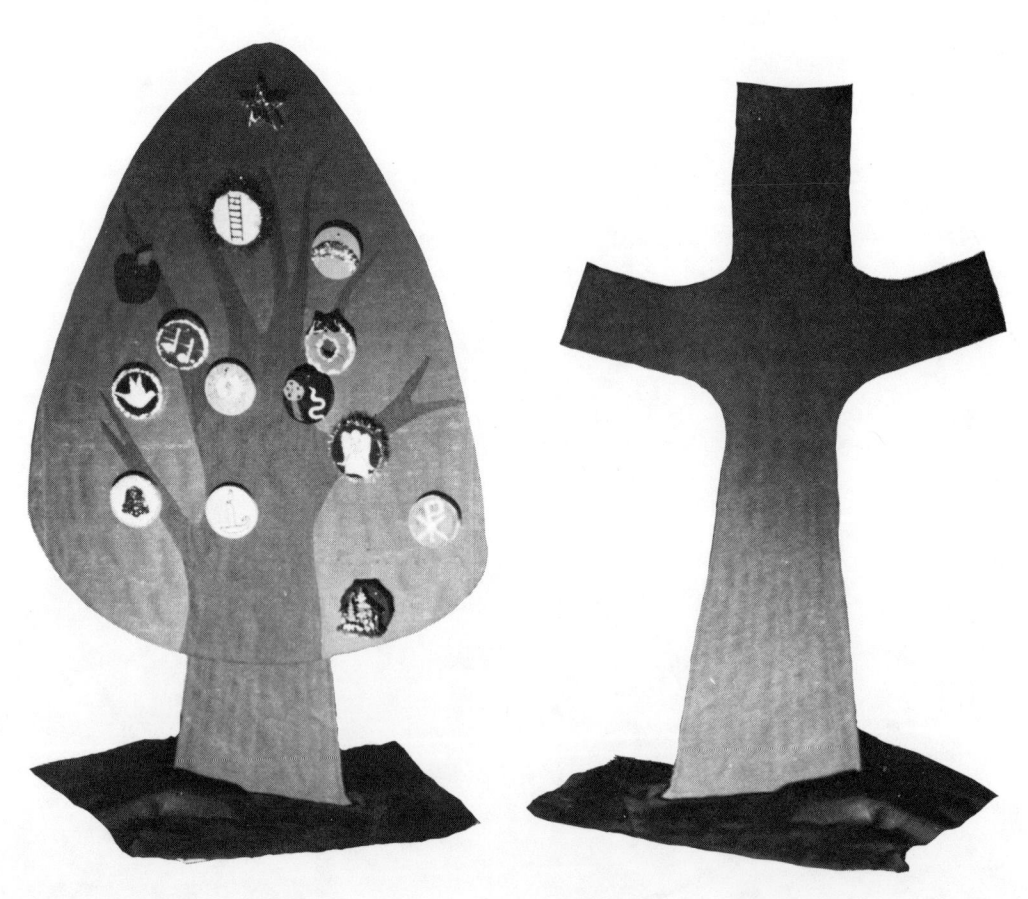

**SYMBOL 1
EVE**

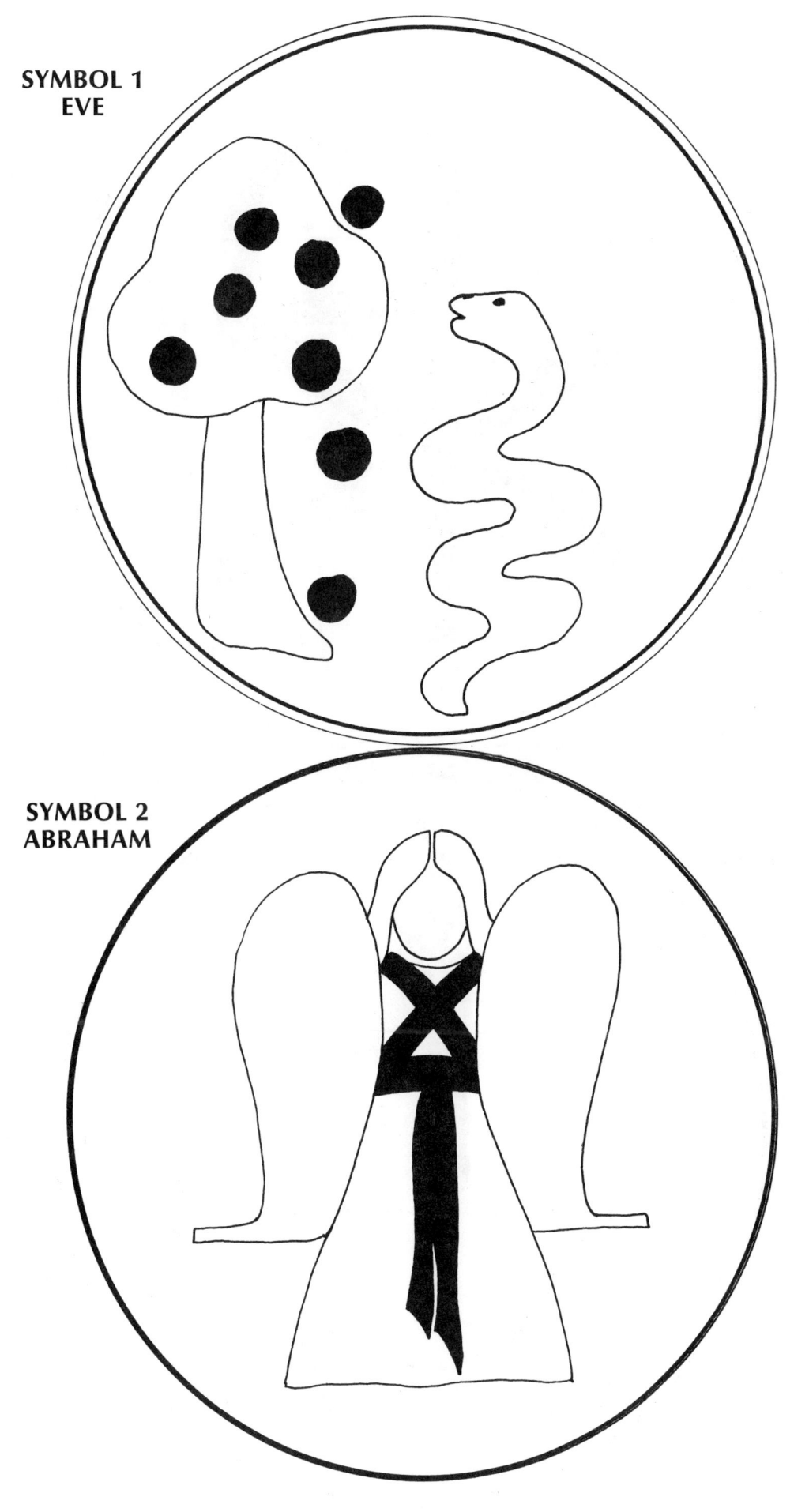

**SYMBOL 2
ABRAHAM**

**SYMBOL 3
JUDAH**

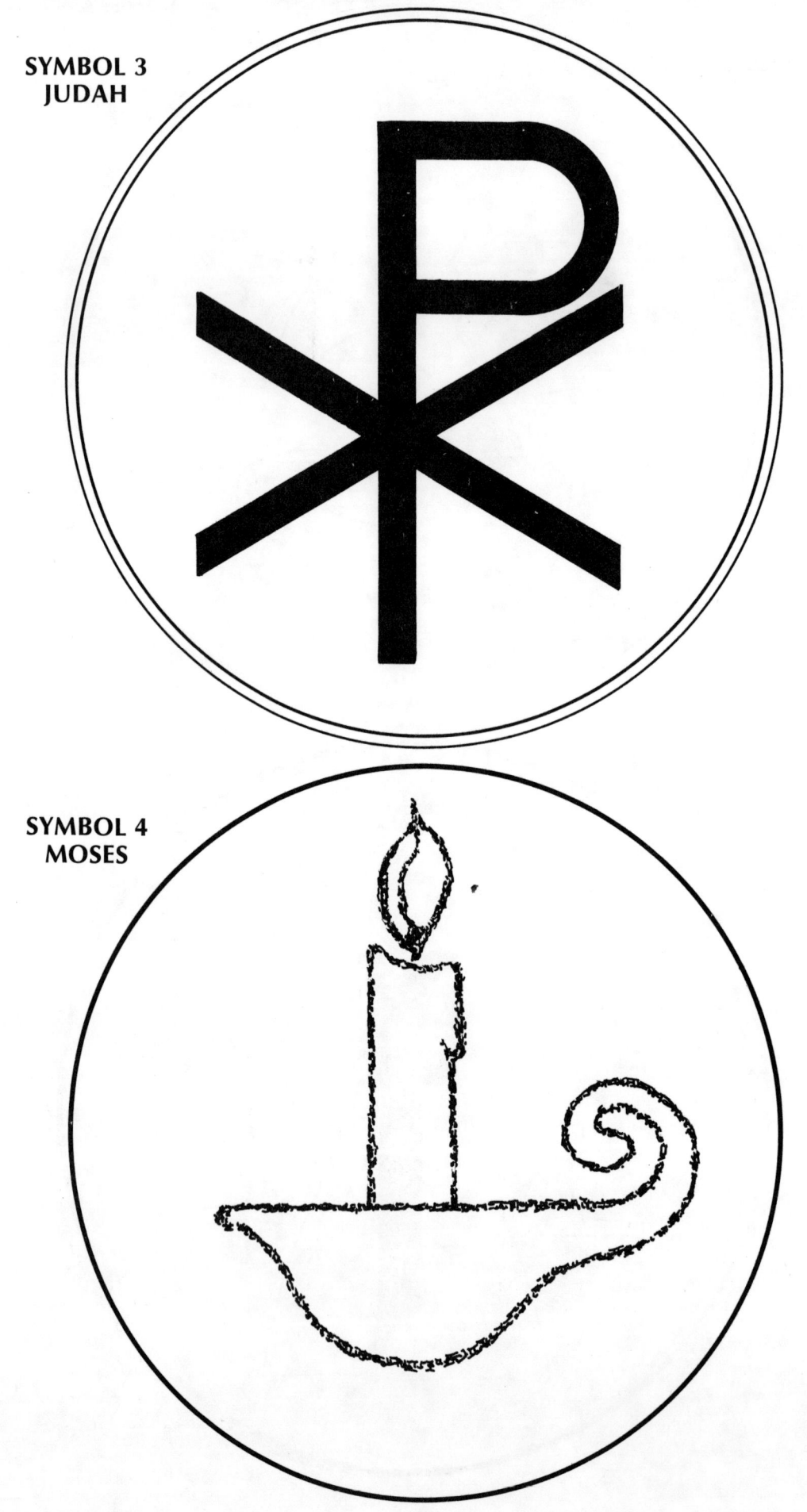

**SYMBOL 4
MOSES**

**SYMBOL 5
DAVID**

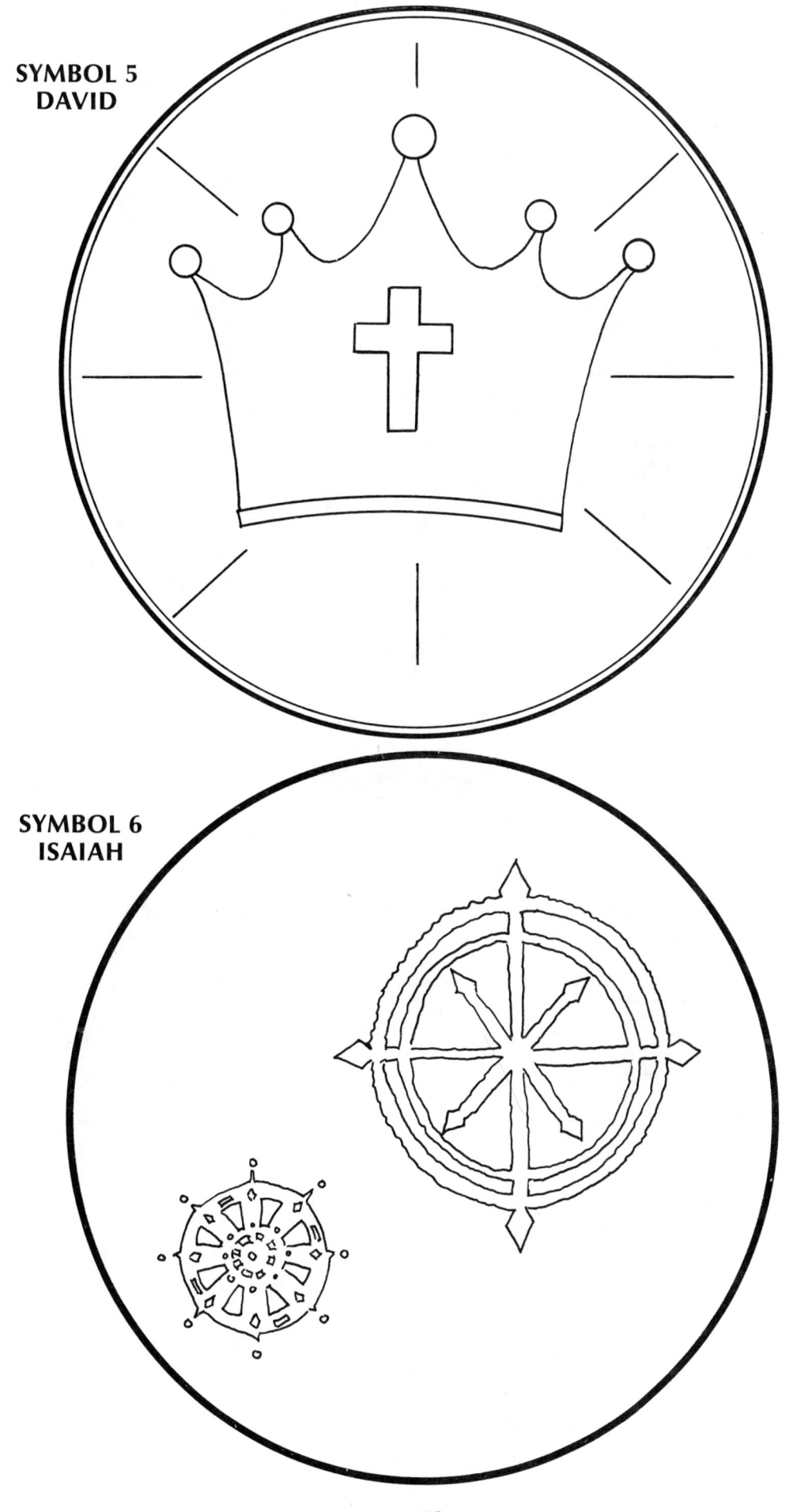

**SYMBOL 6
ISAIAH**

103

**SYMBOL 7
JEREMIAH**

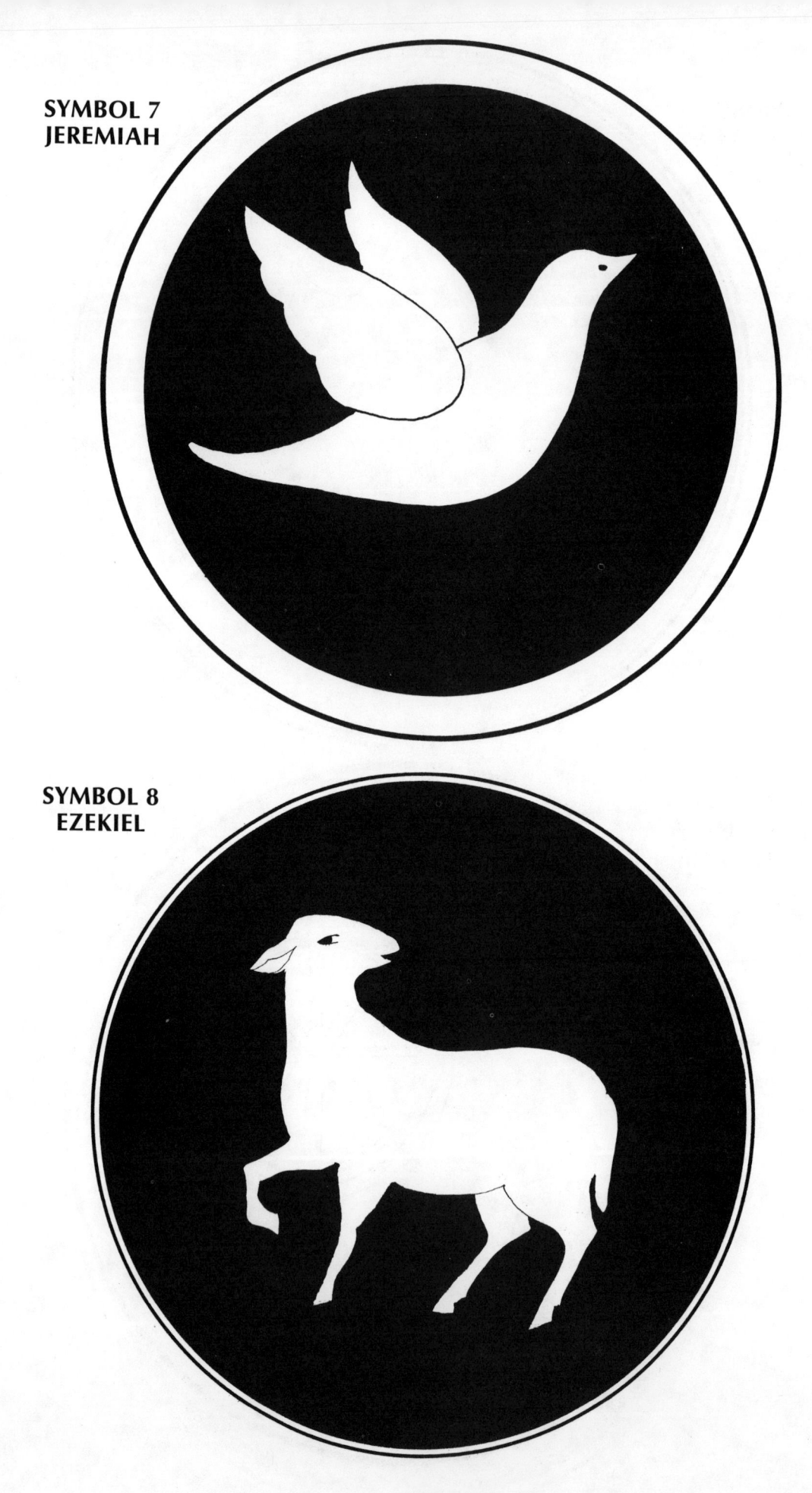

**SYMBOL 8
EZEKIEL**

**SYMBOL 9
DANIEL**

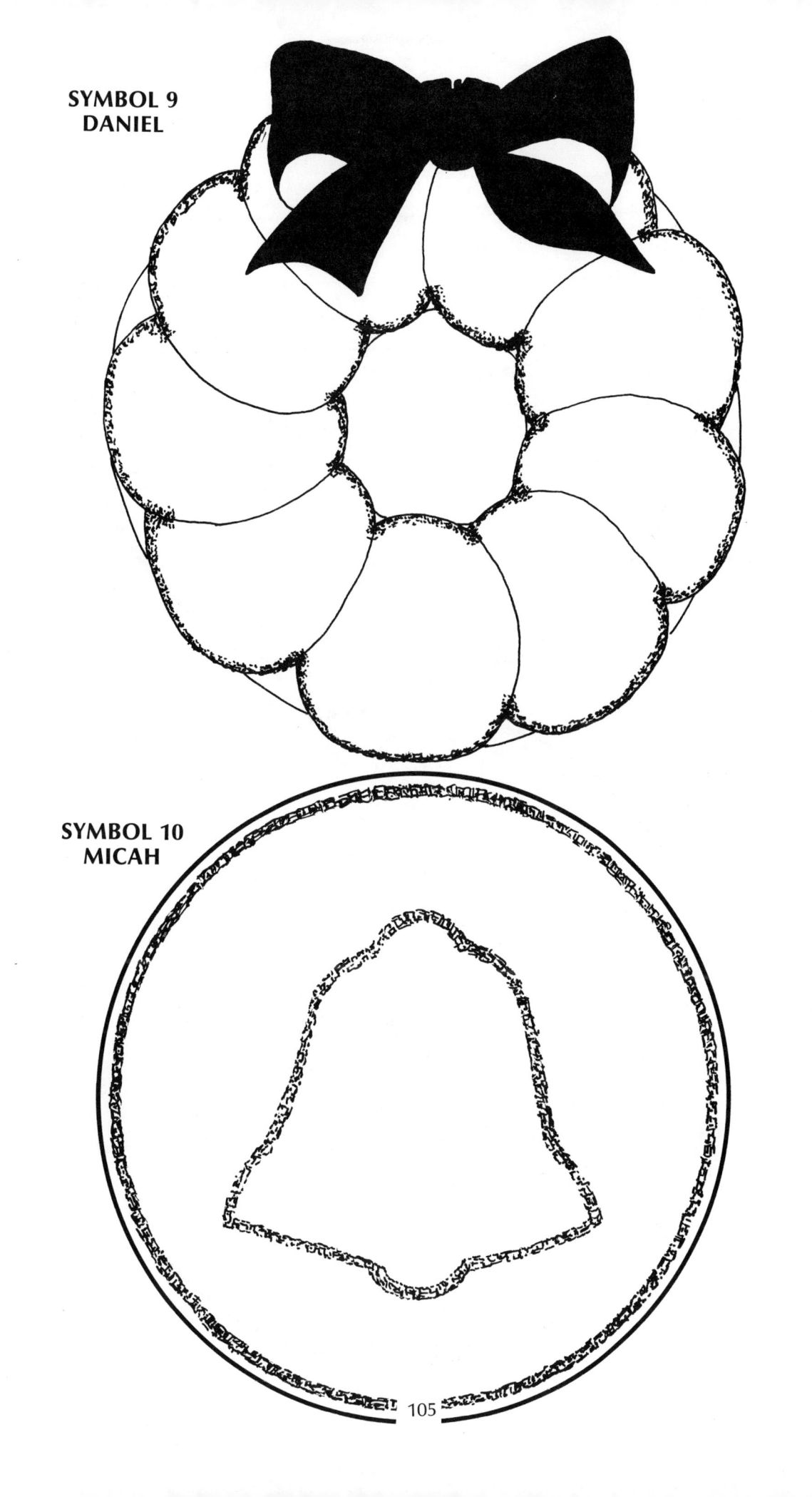

**SYMBOL 10
MICAH**

105

**SYMBOL 11
ZECHARIAH**

**SYMBOL 12
SHEPHERD**

**SYMBOL 13
WISE MAN**

SUGGESTIONS FOR COSTUMES

THE SHEPHERDS

Shepherds' costumes can be made from dark heavy muslin material. The robes may hang loosely or may be belted with leather or cord. Dark-colored blankets can be made into tunics, capes, or shawls.

Shepherds' headdresses can be made from large squares of material (two to three feet square). A strip of material can be sewed on one side of the square for tying it around the shepherd's head and holding it firmly in place. Tie the band at the head and tuck in the loose ends. Let the long end of the headdress hang loosely over the shepherd's neck and shoulders.

SHEPHERD'S HEADDRESS

SHEPHERD'S ROBE

THE WISE MEN

A wide variety of materials may be used to make kingly robes—leftover tapestry, draperies, or colorful materials used for evening wear. The crowns can be made from tagboard and gilded on both sides. Keep them flat and make them long enough so they can be adjusted to various head sizes. Put wax paper between the crowns to preserve them when they are being stored.

CROWN PATTERNS

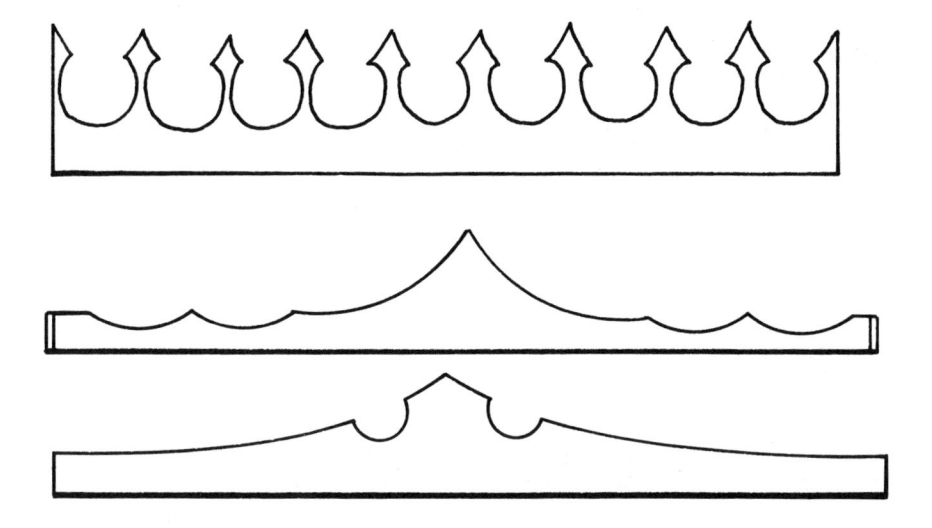

GIFTS OF THE MAGI

For gifts of the Magi use fancy dishes or jewel chests. These may also be made from papier-mâché, clay, or cardboard and sprayed with gold paint.

MARY AND JOSEPH

Mary's costume should be a loosely fitted robe of white or light blue. Her headdress should be draped over her head, around her neck, and over her shoulder. Her cape or shawl can be made from a heavy light-colored material and worn over her shoulders, fastened at the neck.

Joseph's robe and headdress can be similar to that of the shepherds. His robe is often gray and the headdress purple. His shawl can be draped over the right shoulder, across to the left side, and under the arm. It can be secured with a fastener at the shoulder.

HOW TO MAKE ROBES AND TUNICS

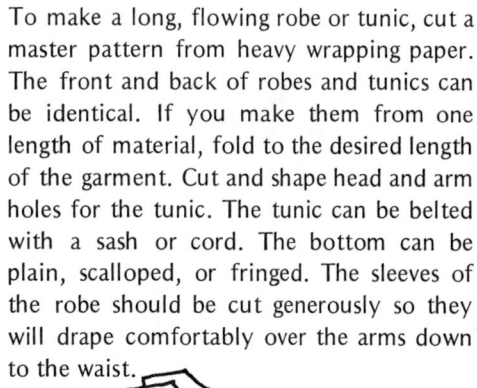

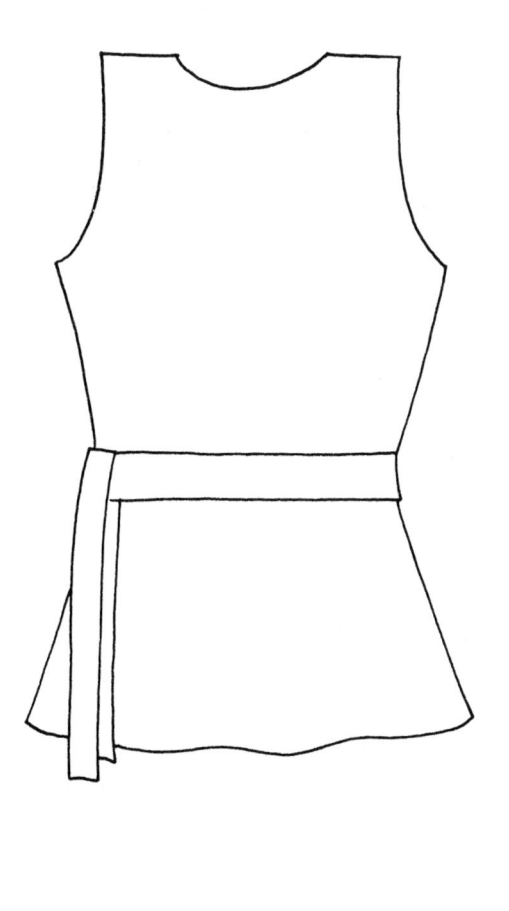

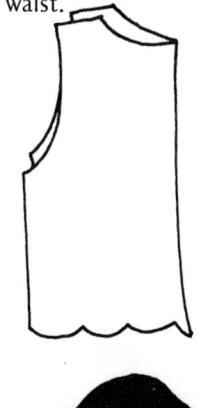

To make a long, flowing robe or tunic, cut a master pattern from heavy wrapping paper. The front and back of robes and tunics can be identical. If you make them from one length of material, fold to the desired length of the garment. Cut and shape head and arm holes for the tunic. The tunic can be belted with a sash or cord. The bottom can be plain, scalloped, or fringed. The sleeves of the robe should be cut generously so they will drape comfortably over the arms down to the waist.

HOW TO MAKE CAPES

A long cape can be made from a yard of material gathered or pleated and attached to a band. Add strings or another type of fastener to tie at the neck. Make two 6-inch slits just above the waistline for the hands. Shorter and different type capes can be made simply by varying the size and shape of the basic pattern.

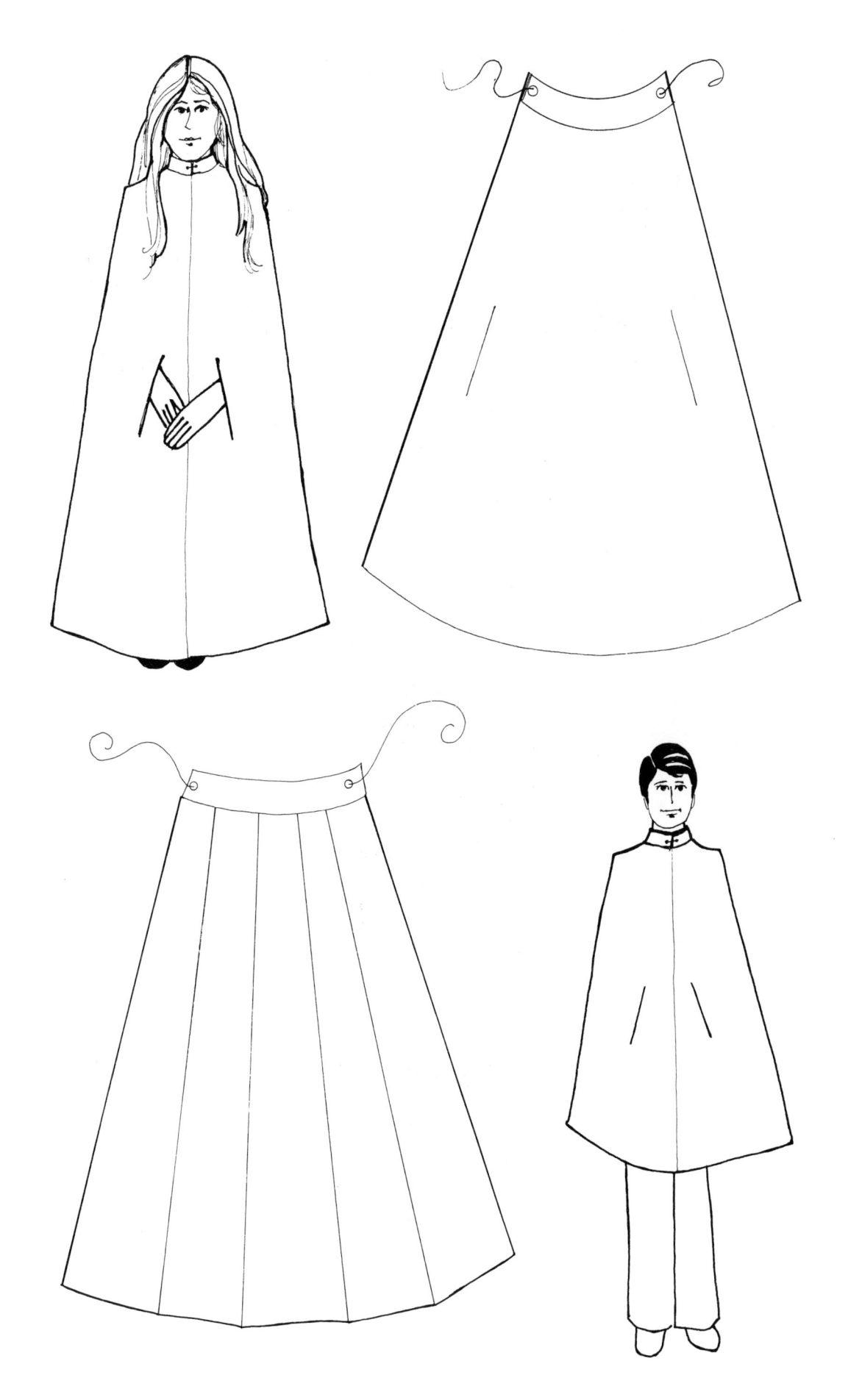

"FLASHLIGHT" CANDLES

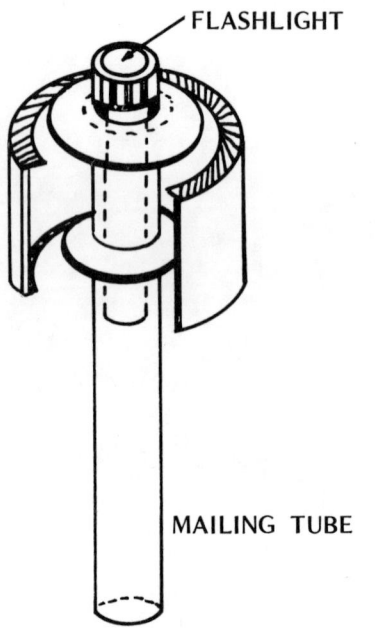

FLASHLIGHT

MAILING TUBE

If battery-operated candles are not available, you can use regular flashlights inserted into cardboard tubes. Cut two disks of cardboard five inches in diameter. Fit the first over the top of the tube. Cut a hole in the other disk large enough to insert the body of the flashlight, but small enough to support the light chamber. Cut a strip of cardboard four inches high with one-inch tabs to go between the two disks. Add tissue on top for a flame.

Part Three
PROGRAMS FOR GROUPS WITHOUT AUDIENCES

ADVENT WREATH PROGRAMS

Jesus Christ is the Light of the World. In the Christmas season, Christians celebrate the birth of Christ. The lighting of the candles of the Advent wreath, remind them that Jesus has come to drive away the darkness of sin.

The two programs that follow are similar in many ways. Both make use of a variety of Scripture references to tell the Christmas story. Both use familiar songs that add to the meaning of the Christmas season. Both are appropriate for use in Advent worship services.

Yet they are different; for the first, **An Advent Celebration,** has more speaking parts and was written with a church school class in mind as the most likely users. The second, **Advent Candle Custom,** makes a broader use of Christmas poetry and has worship within the Christian family as its primary target.

We encourage you to read both programs and select the one that is best suited to the group that will be participating in the service. Parts of the two programs may be used in combination or interchangeably.

If the Advent wreath is placed in the church sanctuary, a different group of church school children may be given the responsibility for lighting the candles and leading the Advent celebration during each of the four weeks prior to Christmas. This allows them to participate in the general church service in a very meaningful way over a period of time rather than simply giving one Christmas program. If this plan is followed, special attention must be given to planning with the minister for the children's participation.

A circle of styrofoam may be used as the base of an Advent wreath. A circular wire molding or wooden frame would work equally well. The size of the wreath may vary according to the space where it will be displayed. Four candles should be equally spaced in the ring and care should be given to insure that they are securely based. Often these candles are violet in color or have bits of purple ribbon tied to them to indicate the royalty or kingship of Christ; however, candles of other colors with special meanings may be used as well. The larger center candle is usually white. Evergreen boughs should be interwoven over the structure of the base and around the candles.

AN ADVENT CELEBRATION

LIGHTING OF THE FIRST CANDLE

Reader One: The people that walked in darkness have seen a great light; on those who dwelt in a land of deep shadow a light has shone.

All: Who will bring light to the world?

Reader Two: Jesus is coming! The promises of the prophets are coming true. Jesus, the Light of the world, is coming to earth!

All: For to us a child is born, to us a son is given; and the government will be upon his shoulders,

Reader Three: And his name will be called Wonderful Counselor, Mighty God, Everlasting Father, Prince of Peace.

All: Jesus, the Light of the world, is coming to earth!

Hymn: O come, O come, Emmanuel,
And ransom captive Israel,
That mourns in lonely exile here,
Until the Son of God appear.

Refrain: Rejoice! Rejoice! Emmanuel
Shall come to thee, O Israel.

O come, Thou Bright and Morning Star,
And bring us comfort from afar!
Dispel the shadows of the night,
And turn our darkness into light.

LIGHTING OF THE SECOND CANDLE

All: The chosen people, Israel, waited for the Light. They waited for many years for God's promise to come true.

Reader One: Then, one day, an angel came down from heaven. He went to visit a young woman named Mary.

Angel One: Do not be afraid, Mary, for you have found favor with God. Behold, you will have a son and you must call him Jesus. He will be great, and will be called the son of the most high; and the Lord will give him the throne of his father David, and he will reign over the house of Jacob forever; And of his kingdom there will be no end.

All: He will be here soon! Christ Jesus will be here soon! The angel has brought the good news!

Hymn: O little town of Bethlehem,
How still we see thee lie!
Above thy deep and dreamless sleep
The silent stars go by.
Yet in thy dark streets shineth

The everlasting Light;
The hopes and fears of all the years
Are met in thee tonight.

LIGHTING OF THE THIRD CANDLE

Reader Two: And in that region there were shepherds out in the field, keeping watch over their flock by night.

Reader Three: And an angel of the Lord appeared to them, and the glory of the Lord shone around them, and they were filled with fear.

Angel Two: Be not afraid; for, behold, I bring you good news of great joy which will come to all the people; for to you is born this day in the city of David, a Savior, who is Christ the Lord. And this will be a sign for you: you will find a babe wrapped in swaddling clothes and lying in a manger.

Reader One: And suddenly there was with the angel a multitude of the heavenly host praising God and saying:

All: "Glory to God in the highest, and on earth peace among men with whom he is pleased."

Shepherd One: I can hardly believe it! Those were angels and they came to talk to *us!*

Shepherd Two: And the news they brought is so wonderful! A Savior has been born! Christ the Lord is here!

Shepherd Three: Quickly! We must go to Bethlehem and see this child that the angels have told us about. We must go and worship!

Readers: He is here! The Light of the world is here!

All: He is here! The Light of the world is here!

Hymn: Silent night! Holy night!
All is calm, all is bright
Round yon virgin mother and Child!
Holy Infant so tender and mild,
Sleep in heavenly peace.

Silent night! Holy night!
Shepherds quake at the sight!
Glories stream from heaven afar,
Heavenly hosts sing: "Alleluia!
Christ the Savior is born!"

LIGHTING OF THE FOURTH CANDLE

Hymn: O come, all ye faithful, joyful and triumphant!
O come ye, O come ye to Bethlehem!
Come and behold Him, born the King of angels.
O come, let us adore Him, Christ the Lord.

Reader One: There was another light that announced the birth of Jesus.

Reader Two:	It was a star so bright and wonderful that wise men, who studied the stars, wondered where a King had been born!
Reader Three:	The wise men were so curious that they traveled many, many miles until they reached the city of Jerusalem.
All:	The three wise men walked up and down the streets of Jerusalem, asking if anyone knew where the newborn King lived.
Reader One:	"We know there is a new King," they said. "We have seen His star and have come to worship Him!"
Reader Two:	Herod was sitting alone in his palace when he heard this news. He began to worry. Who could this *new* King be?
Reader Three:	Herod called in all of the smartest men in his kingdom. They bowed before the angry king and tried to answer his questions. He ordered them to find out if any of the prophets had mentioned the birth of a new king. After much searching, one of the men found the words of a prophet who had lived many, many years before.
All:	And from you, Bethlehem, shall come a ruler Who will govern my people Israel.
Reader One:	When Herod heard these words, he stomped up and down the room. He scratched his beard and clenched his fists. "Call these wise men!" he ordered in a loud, angry voice.
Reader Two:	When the wise men came, Herod got a very sneaky look on his face. He said: "If you find this new King, come back and tell me where He is staying so that I can worship Him too."
Reader Three:	The wise men left Herod's palace. When they were out of the city, one of them pointed excitedly at the star. "There it is again!" he cried. "It will lead us to the newborn King."
All:	At last the three wise men reached the house where the baby Jesus lay. With great happiness, they entered the house, carrying their expensive gifts.
Reader One:	When they saw Jesus, they fell on their knees and worshiped Him, and they offered Him their treasures of gold, frankincense, and myrrh.
Hymn:	What can I give Him, poor as I am? If I were a shepherd, I would give Him a lamb; If I were a Wise Man, I would do my part— But what can I give Him, give my heart.
All:	When the wise men left, they were filled with joy. They had seen the Light! They had seen the King—the Son of God! And warned by God in a dream not to return to King Herod, they departed for their country by another way.

LIGHTING OF THE FIFTH CANDLE

Reader One:	Jesus is in heaven now! He came to earth to die—to save us from our sins!

Reader Two:	That is why He was born in that stable in Bethlehem.
Reader Three:	But Jesus is coming again!
All:	Jesus is coming again!
Reader Three:	He has promised to return!
All:	He who brought us light has promised to return!
Reader One:	We don't know when He is coming, but He will come!
All:	He will come!
Reader Two:	For it says: "But of that day or that hour no one knows, not even the angels in heaven, nor the Son, but only the Father. Take heed, watch; for you do not know when the time will come."
All:	We are watching. We are waiting for our Savior to come again. In this Christmas service we celebrate the first time He came.
Reader Three:	We celebrate His first coming and we wait for Him to come again.
All:	Come quickly, Lord Jesus!
Hymn:	Once in royal David's city Stood a lowly cattle shed, Where a mother laid her Baby In a manger for His bed. Mary was that mother mild, Jesus Christ her little Child. Not in that poor lowly stable With the oxen standing by, We shall see Him, but in heaven, Set at God's right hand on high. When like stars His children crowned All in white shall wait around.
Prayer:	Dear God, We thank You for sending Your Son, Jesus to bring light into our dark world; And we say with Christians all over the earth: Come, thou long-expected Jesus; Born to set Thy people free; From our fears and sins release us; Let us find our rest in Thee. Born Thy people to deliver, Born a Child, and yet a King, Born to reign in us forever, Now Thy gracious kingdom bring. Come quickly, Lord Jesus! Amen.

ADVENT CANDLE CUSTOM

Shortly after the Christian church established December 25 as the date to celebrate Christmas, Christians felt the need to prepare themselves spiritually for Christmas. Thus they started the custom of the Advent candles. To observe that custom the Christian family places four candles in a simple wreath of evergreens. In the center of the wreath they place a fifth candle that is taller than the others. Then they put the wreath in an important place in the home.

On each of the four Sundays before Christmas and on Christmas Day the family gathers for Bible reading and song. On the first Sunday one of the smaller candles is lit—often by the youngest child. On the next Sunday another child relights the first and also lights a second candle. The family repeats this ceremony each Sunday until all the candles are lit on Christmas Day. The taller, center candle, sometimes called the "Jesus Candle," is lit last. It represents the focus of the Christian celebration of Christmas—the Christ child.

Some families use different colored candles to represent different ideas. Many Advent services are based primarily on Old Testament Bible passages. The purpose is always, however, to help a Christian family prepare for Christmas. The selections center on simple but important themes. Familiar songs are chosen so that even the youngest children can participate.

FIRST SUNDAY IN ADVENT

Hymn:
O come, O come, Emmanuel,
And ransom captive Israel,
That mourns in lonely exile here,
Until the Son of God appear.

Rejoice! Rejoice! Emmanuel
Shall come to thee, O Israel.

O, come, Thou Bright and Morning Star,
And bring us comfort from afar!
Dispel the shadows of the night,
And turn our darkness into light.

Candle-lighting Theme: Jesus is the light of the world.

Hymn:
O little town of Bethlehem,
How still we see thee lie!
Above thy deep and dreamless sleep
The silent stars go by.
Yet in the dark streets shineth
The everlasting light;
The hopes and fears of all the years
Are met in thee tonight.

For Christ is born of Mary,
And gathered all above,
While mortals sleep, the angels keep
Their watch of wondering love.
O morning stars, together
Proclaim the holy birth!
And praises sing to God the King,
And peace to men on earth.

Scripture: Isaiah 9:2, 6, 7

Prayer: Out of my bondage, sorrow and night,
Jesus, I come, Jesus, I come;
Into Thy freedom, gladness and light,
Jesus, I come to Thee.
Out of my sickness into Thy health,
Out of my want and into Thy wealth,
Out of my sin and into Thyself,
Jesus, I come to Thee. Amen.

Hymn: Come, Thou long-expected Jesus,
Born to set Thy people free;
From our fears and sins release us;
Let us find our rest in Thee.

Born Thy people to deliver,
Born a Child, and yet a King,
Born to reign in us forever,
Now Thy gracious Kingdom bring. Amen.

SECOND SUNDAY IN ADVENT

Hymn: Angels, from the realms of glory,
Wing your flight o'er all the earth;
Ye who sang creation's story,
Now proclaim Messiah's birth.
Come and worship, come and worship,
Worship Christ, the new-born King.

Candle-lighting Theme: The angel Gabriel announces to Mary that she will be the mother of Jesus.

Scripture: Luke 1:26-38

Poem: This is the month, and this the happy morn,
Wherein the Son of Heaven's Eternal King,
Of wedded maid and virgin mother born,
Our great redemption from above did bring;
For so the holy sages once did sing,
That he our deadly forfeit should release,
And with his Father work us a perpetual peace.

Prayer: Come Jesus, holy Child, to me;
Close tight my heart to all but Thee;
And with Thy Holy Spirit's grace
Make me, dear Lord, Thy dwelling place.

With joy and love I wait for Thee
To come with Thy good gifts to me.
Stay close to me through all my days;
Then let me sing in heaven Thy praise.
   Amen.
      Musae Sioniae, tr. by Paul Z. Strodach

Hymn: My soul doth magnify the Lord;
In Him my spirit doth rejoice,

For He beheld my low estate,
And in His love made me His choice.
   Amen.

THIRD SUNDAY IN ADVENT

Hymn: Oh, leave your sheep, you shepherds
            on the hills,
Leave fields and rocks, and all the
            care of flocks.
Your sorrow deep now change to joy
            that thrills;
Come hither and adore your God, your
            God, who heals your grief so sore.

Candle-lighting Theme: The angels tell the shepherds that Jesus is born.

Scripture: Luke 2:1-20

Poem: I saw the sky grow strangely bright,
Heard angel voices in the night,
But I have never bothered much
With angel songs and stars and such;
Through all the countryside it's said
I've always kept a steady head.
What kind of shepherd leaves his sheep?
Remember—we had flocks to keep.

And I for duty had a mind,
So I alone remained behind.
That visit made them different men—
They never seemed the same again—
But I can't understand the plan
How God himself became a man.

It happened years ago and yet
It's something that I can't forget.
I try to push the thought away—
But I suppose it's there to stay.

If angels came to sing again,
Perhaps I'd seek the Christ-Child then;
At least I'd satisfy my doubt
And learn what this is all about,
And I would make a change in me.
But I am old and soon to die;
No doubt my chance has passed me by;
And I have never bothered much
With angel songs and stars and such.

Prayer: Welcome to earth, Thou noble Guest
Through whom the sinful world is blest.
Thou com'st to share my misery;
What thanks shall I return to Thee?

Ah, dearest Jesus, holy Child,
Make Thee a bed, soft, undefiled,

	Within my heart, that it may be
	A quiet chamber kept for Thee. Amen.
Hymn:	Away in a manger, no crib for a bed,
	The little Lord Jesus laid down His sweet head.
	The stars in the sky looked down where He lay,
	The little Lord Jesus asleep on the hay.

FOURTH SUNDAY IN ADVENT

Hymn:	O come, all ye faithful, joyful, and triumphant;
	O come ye, O come ye to Bethlehem.
	Come and behold Him, born the King of angels;
	O come, let us adore Him, Christ the Lord.
Candle-lighting Theme:	Some wise men follow a star to find the baby Jesus.
Scripture:	Matthew 2:1-12
Poem:	The shepherds had an angel,
	The wise men had a star,
	But what have I, a little child,
	To guide me home from far,
	Where glad stars sing together,
	And singing angels are?
	Lord Jesus is my guardian,
	So I can nothing lack;
	The lambs lie in His bosom
	Along life's dangerous track:
	The willful lambs that go astray
	He bleeding fetches back....
	The wise men left their country
	To journey morn by morn,
	With gold and frankincense and myrrh,
	Because the Lord was born:
	God sent a star to guide them
	And sent a dream to warn.
	My life is like their journey,
	Their star is like God's book;
	I must be like those good wise men
	With heavenward heart and look.
Prayer:	As with gladness men of old
	Did the guiding star behold,
	As with joy they hailed its light,
	Leading onward, beaming bright,
	So, most gracious God, may we
	Evermore be led to Thee.

          Holy Jesus! every day
          Keep us in the narrow way.
          And, when earthly things are past,
          Bring our ransomed souls at last
          Where they need no star to guide,
          Where no clouds Thy glory hide. Amen.

Hymn: What can I give Him, poor as I am?
If I were a shepherd, I would give a lamb;
If I were a Wise Man, I would do my part—
But what can I give Him, give my heart. Amen.

CHRISTMAS DAY

Hymn: Let our gladness know no end,
    Hallelujah!
Unto earth did Christ descend,
    Hallelujah!
Into flesh is made the Word,
    Hallelujah!
He our refuge and our Lord,
    Hallelujah!

On this day God gave us
Christ, His Son, to save us,
Gave us Christ, His Son, to save us.

Candle-lighting Theme: Jesus is coming again.

Scripture: Mark 13:24-27; 32-37

Hymn: Once in royal David's city
Stood a lowly cattle shed,
Where a mother laid her Baby
In a manger for His bed.
Mary was that mother mild,
Jesus Christ her little Child.

Not in that poor lowly stable
With the oxen standing by,
We shall see Him, but in heaven,
Set at God's right hand on high,
When like stars His children crowned
All in white shall wait around.

Prayer: Savior, hasten Thine appearing,
Bring, O bring the glorious day
When, the awful summons hearing,
Heaven and earth shall pass away;
Then with golden harp, we'll sing,
Glory, glory to our King! Amen.

Hymn: Come, Thou long-expected Jesus,
Born to set Thy people free;

From our fears and sins release us;
Let us find our rest in Thee.

Born Thy people to deliver,
Born a Child, and yet a King,
Born to reign in us forever,
Now Thy gracious kingdom bring. Amen.

National Union of Christian Schools,
Revelation Response Series,
"God's Witnesses," pp. 61-66.

THE FULLNESS OF TIME

Prelude: "O Come, All Ye Faithful"

First Reader: "The Fullness of Time." Do you know who first said these words? There is a ring of mystery about them. They speak of God's preparation for Christmas.

Second Reader: Have you ever wondered what it would be like to have lived in Bethlehem when Christ was born? What if Jesus had been born at a different time or place? As you prepare for Christmas this year I want you to see how God prepared the world for Christ's coming.

Song: "Joy to the World!"

Second Reader: There were three groups of people with whom God had worked to get ready for Jesus' birth.

First Reader: (Read Luke 2:1) Caesar Augustus was king of the Roman people. The Romans had provided a modern system of roads and highways. There was a just system of laws and government. At the time Jesus was born there was peace on earth. However, sex and sadism created a superficial society. People needed someone to give meaning and depth to life. Would it be a politician, a judge, or a great prophet?

Second Reader: The Greeks' contribution toward God's preparation was their language. The tradesmen spoke Greek in the market place. The strivings of men for knowledge and wisdom were recorded in this language. But at this time the Greek philosophers realized they lacked solutions to many problems. Who would be next on the scene? Would it be an educator, a lecturer, or an essayist? Would he have the answers?

Song: "Come, Thou Long-expected Jesus"

First Reader: Then there was a third group of people who assisted in God's preparation to make it "the fullness of time." They were the Jews. At this time they were scattered in different countries. The Roman government permitted them to worship their Jehovah God. They spoke of Him at the market place or the city well. The Samaritan woman said, "I know that Messiah cometh, which is called Christ: when he is come, he will declare unto us all things." They all groaned under the yoke of the law. They needed someone to deliver them from their system of salvation by works. Would the Messiah say to them, "Come unto me"? (Read Matthew 11:28-30.)

Song: "O Come, O Come, Emmanuel"

Second Reader: God's preparation was completed. The gospel would be able to go forth. Jesus and His disciples would be free to travel from one country to another because of good roads. Visas were unnecessary, thanks to a world-embracing government. They wouldn't have to spend six months to two years learning another language as our missionaries do today, for in all the lands of the Roman Empire there were people who could speak and understand Greek.

First Reader: God's ways are wonderful. A world power had to cooperate. And a decree went forth. (Read Luke 2:1, 3, 4.)

Second Reader:	In the fullness of time prophecy was fulfilled. Now things happened. Mary and Joseph headed south. Strange wonder occupied their minds; many questions crowded their hearts! (Read Psalm 98.)
Song:	"O Little Town of Bethlehem"
First Reader:	Soon the lights of Bethlehem could be seen. Then the sad note sounded.
Second Reader:	"Sorry, no room—you'll have to go some other place, we have only a stable." *(pause)* It was good enough—Mary was tired.
Song:	"Silent Night"
First Reader:	Read Luke 2:6, 7.
Second Reader:	The world would never be the same. Morals would be lifted, answers would be given, peace would reign in men's hearts. Because "God sent forth his Son, born of a woman, born under the law, . . . that we might receive the adoption of sons." God determined the evening. Bethlehem was the right town, the manger was the intended bed!
First Reader:	Thou didst for all prepare This Gift, so great, so rare, That peoples might adore Thee; A light to show the way To nations gone astray, And unto Israel's glory.
Song:	"Hark! the Herald Angels Sing"

Ida Gunnink

A CHRISTMAS DEVOTIONAL

Narrator: Come, all ye faithful, come, let us adore Him, Christ the Lord.

Song: "O Come, All Ye Faithful"

Narrator: This is the Lord and Christ of whom the ancient prophets spoke. This is the Savior longed for from the days of Abraham and of the tabernacle and of the long captivity. In those centuries God raised up His messengers and prophets to speak about the Savior-King who was to come. It was the weeping prophet Jeremiah who spoke these words from God:

Speaking Choir: "Behold, the days are coming, says the Lord, when I will raise up for David a righteous Branch, and he shall reign as king and deal wisely, and shall execute justice and righteousness in the land.... And this is the name by which he will be called: 'The Lord is our righteousness.'" (Jeremiah 23:5, 6b)

Narrator: Malachi, prophesying in the days of Nehemiah when the Persians ruled the Jewish people, said:

Speaking Choir: "Behold, I send my messengers to prepare the way before me, and the Lord whom you seek will suddenly come to his temple; the messenger of the covenant in whom you delight, behold, he is coming, says the Lord of hosts." (Malachi 3:1)

Narrator: Micah, the peasant prophet, spoke great things about a little town.

Speaking Choir: "But you, O Bethlehem Ephratah, who are little to be among the clans of Judah, from you shall come forth for me one who is to be ruler in Israel, whose origin is from of old, from everlasting." (Micah 5:2)

Narrator: And Isaiah, that great prophet through whom God spoke most clearly about the Savior, cried out triumphantly:

Speaking Choir: "The people who walked in darkness have seen a great light.... For unto us a child is born, unto us a son is given; and the government shall be upon his shoulder, and his name shall be called Wonderful, Counselor, Mighty God, Everlasting Father, Prince of Peace." (Isaiah 9:2, 6)

Song: "O Come, O Come, Emmanuel"

Narrator: "And when the time had fully come, God sent forth his Son, born of woman, born under the law, to redeem those who were under the law, so that we might receive adoption as sons" (Galatians 4:4, 5). All the history of the world had been moving toward the coming of God's Son. And even Caesar Augustus from his palace in Rome was used to make the prophecies come true. This is how it happened.

Speaking Choir: In those days a decree went out from Caesar Augustus that all the world should be enrolled. This was the first enrollment, when Quirinius was governor of Syria. And all went to be enrolled, each to his own city. And Joseph also went up from Galilee, from the city of Nazareth, to Judea, to the city of David, which is called Bethlehem, because he was of the house and lineage of David, to be enrolled with Mary, his betrothed, who was

	with child. And while they were there, the time came for her to be delivered. And she gave birth to her firstborn son and wrapped him in swaddling cloths, and laid him in a manger, because there was no place for them in the inn."
Song:	"Silent Night"
Narrator:	Not to the king in Jerusalem, but to shepherds keeping watch in the open fields God sent announcement by His angels.
Song:	"While Shepherds Watched Their Flocks by Night"
Speaking Choir:	"When the angels went away from them into heaven, the shepherds said one to another, Let us go over to Bethlehem and see this thing that has happened, which the Lord has made known to us. And they went with haste, and found Mary and Joseph, and the baby lying in the manger. And when they saw it they made known the saying which had been told them concerning this child."
Narrator:	And this is God's will concerning the Savior born in Bethlehem, that the news of His coming should still be made known even as the shepherds made it known when they had seen the Child. For this is the good news of all the ages, that God did keep His promise made through prophets, and that the Savior of the world had come. And we have more to tell than shepherds did. For we have God's own written story of the Savior's life and death. From the pages of the Bible we can hear Christ speaking to us as He spoke to His disciples and to Martha.
Speaking Choir:	"I am the way, and the truth, and the life; no one comes to the Father, but by me. . . . I am the resurrection and the life; he who believes in me, though he die, yet shall he live; and whosoever lives and believes in me shall never die."
Narrator:	This is our joy at Christmas—that God's gift to us is a Savior who was born and lived and died for us, who is risen from the dead and ascended into heaven for us, and who will come again to take us to be with Him forever.
Speaking Choir:	Dear Lord Jesus, at this Christmastime Prepare our hearts to receive Thee, Prepare our hands to serve Thee, Prepare our mouths to speak for Thee, And may the great joy of Thy coming be with us now and always. Amen.

Thea B. Van Halsema

Part Four
RECITATIONS

A CHILD'S OFFERING

The wise may bring their learning,
    The rich may bring their wealth,
And some may bring their greatness,
    And some bring strength and health;
We, too, would bring our treasures
    To offer to the King;
We have no wealth or learning:
    What shall we children bring?

We'll bring Him hearts that love Him;
    We'll bring Him thankful praise,
And young souls meekly striving
    To walk in holy ways:
And these shall be the treasures
    We offer to the King,
And these are gifts that even
    The poorest child may bring.

We'll bring the little duties
    We have to do each day;
We'll try our best to please Him,
    At home, at school, at play:
And better are these treasures
    To offer to our King,
Than richest gifts without them;
    Yet these a child may bring.

The Book of Praise for Children, 1881

THAT HOLY STAR

O Father, may that holy star
    Grow every year more bright
And send its glorious beams afar
    To fill the world with light.

William Cullen Bryant

IN THINE OWN HEART

Though Christ a thousand times
    In Bethlehem be born,
If He's not born in thee
    Thy soul is still forlorn.
The cross on Golgotha
    Will never save thy soul,
The cross in thine own heart
    Alone can make thee whole.

From the German of Angelus Silesius, 1624-1677

MY GIFT

What can I give Him
Poor as I am?
If I were a shepherd,
I would give Him a lamb,
If I were a Wise Man,
I would do my part—
But what I can I give Him,
Give my heart.

From "A Christmas Carol" by Christina Rossetti, 1830-1894

A CHRISTMAS VERSE

The wondrous love and light,
   The fullness and the glory,
The meaning and the might
   Of all the Christmas story,
May Christ Himself unfold to you today,
   And bid you go rejoicing on your way.

A happy, happy Christmas,
   Be yours today!
Oh, not the failing measure
   Of fleeting earthly pleasure,
But Christmas joy abiding,
   While years are swiftly gliding,
Be yours, I pray,
   Through Him who gave us Christmas Day.

                Frances Ridley Havergal
           (From *A Chronicle of Christmas*
             by Jeannette Grace Watson)

THE SONG OF MARY

My soul doth magnify the Lord,
   And my spirit hath rejoiced in God my Saviour.
For he hath regarded the low estate of his handmaiden:
   for, behold, from henceforth all generations shall
   call me blessed.
For he that is mighty hath done to me great things;
   and holy is his name.
And his mercy is on them that fear him from
   generation to generation.
He hath shewed strength with his arm;
   he hath scattered the proud in the imagination
   of their hearts.
He hath put down the mighty from their seats,
   and exalted them of low degree.
He hath filled the hungry with good things;
   and the rich he hath sent empty away.
He hath holpen his servant Israel,
   in remembrance of his mercy.
As he spake to our fathers, to Abraham,
   and to his seed for ever.

                Luke 1:46-55, KJV

I HAVE A LITTLE SECRET

Sh-sh-sh! It's nearly Christmas;
   I won't let out a peep.
I have a little secret
   That I am going to keep.

Don't ask a single question,
   Just wait for Christmas Day!
And then I'll take my secret out
   And give it right away.

      Author unknown

HARK, THE GLAD SOUND

Hark, the glad sound! the Savior comes,
    The Savior promised long;
Let every heart prepare a throne,
    And every voice a song!

He comes, the prisoners to release
    In Satan's bondage held;
The gates of brass before Him burst,
    The iron fetters yield.

He comes, the broken heart to bind,
    The bleeding soul to cure,
And with the treasure of His grace
    T'enrich the humble poor.

Our glad hosannas, Prince of Peace,
    Thy welcome shall proclaim,
And heaven's eternal arches ring
    With Thy beloved name.

Philip Doddridge
(From *A Chronicle of Christmas*
by Jeannette Grace Watson)

THE FRIENDLY BEASTS

Jesus our brother, strong and good,
Was humbly born in a stable rude,
And the friendly beasts around Him stood,
Jesus our brother, strong and good.

"I," said the donkey shaggy and brown,
"I carried His mother up hill and down,
I carried her safely to Bethlehem town;
I," said the donkey shaggy and brown.

"I," said the cow all white and red,
"I gave Him my manger for His bed,
I gave Him my hay to pillow His head,
I," said the cow all white and red.

"I," said the sheep with curly horn,
"I gave Him my wool for His blanket warm,
He wore my coat on Christmas morn;
I," said the sheep with curly horn.

"I," said the dove, from the rafters high,
"Cooed Him to sleep, my mate and I;
We cooed Him to sleep, my mate and I;
I," said the dove, from the rafters high.

And every beast, by some good spell,
In the stable dark was glad to tell,
Of the gift he gave Immanuel,
The gift he gave Immanuel.

Twelfth-Century Carol

THE THREE KINGS

Three Kings came riding from far away,
    Melchior and Gaspar and Baltasar;
Three Wise Men out of the East were they,
And they traveled by night and they slept by day,
    For their guide was a beautiful, wonderful star.

The star was so beautiful, large, and clear,
    That all the other stars of the sky
Became a white mist in the atmosphere,
And by this they knew that the coming was near
    Of the Prince foretold in the prophecy.

Three caskets they bore on their saddle-bows,
    Three caskets of gold with golden keys;
Their robes were of crimson silk with rows
Of bells and pomegranates and furbelows,
    Their turbans like blossoming almond-trees.

And so the Three Kings rode into the West,
    Through the dusk of night, over hill and dell,
And sometimes they nodded with beard on breast,
And sometimes they talked, as they paused to rest,
    With the people they met at some wayside well.

"Of the child that is born," said Baltasar,
    "Good people, I pray you, tell us the news;
For we in the East have seen his star,
And have ridden fast, and have ridden far,
    To find and worship the King of the Jews."

And the people answered, "You ask in vain;
    We know of no king but Herod the Great!"
They thought the Wise Men were men insane,
As they spurred their horses across the plain,
    Like riders in haste, and who cannot wait.

And when they came to Jerusalem,
    Herod the Great, who had heard this thing,
Sent for the Wise Men and questioned them;
And said, "Go down unto Bethlehem,
    And bring me tidings of this new king."

So they rode away; and the star stood still,
    The only one in the gray of morn;
Yes, it stopped,—it stood still of its own free will,
Right over Bethlehem on the hill,
    The city of David, where Christ was born.

And the Three Kings rode through the gate and the guard,
    Through the silent street, till their horses turned
And neighed as they entered the great inn-yard;
But the windows were closed, and the doors were barred,
    And only a light in the stable burned.

And cradled there in the scented hay,
    In the air made sweet by the breath of kine,
The little child in the manger lay,
The child, that would be king one day
    Of a kingdom not human but divine.

His mother Mary of Nazareth
    Sat watching beside his place of rest,
Watching the even flow of his breath,
For the joy of life and the terror of death
    Were mingled together in her breast.

They laid their offerings at his feet:
    The gold was their tribute to a King,
The frankincense, with its odor sweet,
Was for the Priest, the Paraclete,
    The myrrh for the body's burying.

And the mother wondered and bowed her head,
    And sat as still as a statue of stone;
Her heart was troubled yet comforted,
Remembering what the Angel had said
    Of an endless reign and of David's throne.

Then the Kings rode out of the city gate,
    With a clatter of hoofs in proud array;
But they went not back to Herod the Great,
For they knew his malice and feared his hate,
    And returned to their homes by another way.

                      Henry Wadsworth Longfellow

LONG, LONG AGO

Winds thru the olive trees
    Softly did blow
Round little Bethlehem
    Long, long ago.

Sheep on the hillside lay
    Whiter than snow
Shepherds were watching them
    Long, long ago.

Then from the happy sky,
    Angels bent low
Singing their songs of joy,
    Long, long ago.

For in a manger bed,
    Cradled we know
Christ came to Bethlehem
    Long, long ago.

Author unknown

CHRISTMAS

Come all you faithful Christians that dwell here on earth,
Come celebrate the morning of our dear Savior's birth.
This is the happy morning, this is the blessed morn!
To save our souls from ruin, the Son of God was born.

Behold the angel Gabriel, in Scripture it is said,
Did with his holy message come to the virgin maid;
Hail, blest among all women! he thus did greet her then,
Lo thou shalt be the mother of the Savior of all men.

Her time being accomplished, she came to Bethlehem.
And then was safe delivered of the Savior of all men.
No princely pomp attended him. His honors were but small:
A manger was his cradle, his bed an ox's stall.

Now to him that is ascended let all our praises be;
May we his steps then follow, and he our pattern be.
So when our lives are ended, we all may hear him call—
Come souls, receive the kingdom, prepared for you all.

Words of traditional Hereford Carol
Copyright 1920 by Stainer & Bell Ltd.

Part Five

EXERCISES

CHRIST'S BIRTH: THE CENTRAL DATE IN HISTORY
(an exercise for intermediate grades)

(First and second speakers, holding between them a poster with the words, BIRTH OF CHRIST, come to stand in the center of the platform.)

First Speaker: On that night long ago when Jesus was born, there was no room in the inn. The innkeeper who offered his stable as a shelter to Mary and Joseph that Christmas night did not know that the child who was to be born and to sleep in a manger there was the Lord of lords and the King of kings. And yet the birth of Christ is the most important date, the central date in history.

Second Speaker: Whether the twenty-fifth day of December which we now observe as Christmas Day is actually the day on which Christ was born is not absolutely certain. During the sixth century, a Roman monk named Dionysius established that Christ was born in the 753rd year of Rome. This year he called 1 A.D., that is, the first "year of our Lord." In the sixteenth century a more careful study showed that Dionysius had made a mistake of about four years in his calculations, for Jesus was born in Bethlehem of Judea before the death of Herod and it was now established that Herod died in the 750th year of Rome just before the feast of the Passover. Because of this mistake, we must keep in mind that Christ was born about the year 4 B.C. in terms of our present calendar.

(Third and fourth speakers enter to stand to the right of the first and second speakers. They hold between them a poster with large letters, B.C.)

Third Speaker: The letters "B.C." stand for the words *Before Christ*. When we talk about events that occurred before Christ was born, we give the date and then add the words *Before Christ*. If we write the date, we add the letters "B.C." For example, Abraham lived about 2000 years B.C.; Moses lived about 1400 B.C.; Solomon built the temple about 970 B.C.

Fourth Speaker: The last book of the Old Testament, Malachi, was written about 400 B.C. None of the people who lived before Christ was born could celebrate Christmas Day as we are able to do. They could only look forward to the time that Christ was born. It must have been much harder to have faith in those days than it is today. They had to believe that in the fullness of time, God would keep His promises and send the Messiah. Our calendar helps us to remember that Christ has come.

(Fifth and sixth speakers enter to stand to the left of the first and second speakers. They hold between them a poster with the large letters, A.D.)

Fifth Speaker: The letters "A.D." stand for the Latin words *Anno Domini*, which mean "In the Year of Our Lord" or "After Christ." Every time we celebrate New Year's Day, in fact, every time we wrote 19____ during the year that is almost past, we were reminding ourselves that we are living one thousand nine hundred _____ years after the birth of Christ. Although it would be correct and proper to write A.D. each time we write the date, we seldom do so, except on official historical documents.

Sixth Speaker: The dates we use to designate the years before Christ grow smaller and smaller as they approach the date when Christ was born. The number of the years on our calendar grows larger and larger. For example, Jesus was crucified about 30 A.D.; the apostle Paul was converted about 38 A.D.; Constantine, who helped to spread Christianity in Europe lived about 300 A.D.; Martin Luther nailed his ninety-five theses to the door of the Castle Church in Wittenberg in 1517 A.D; and we are living in the year 19—A.D.

First Speaker: All of the dates of history before Christ's birth pointed forward to the time of His coming.

Second Speaker: All of the dates of history since the first Christmas long ago remind us that we are living in the Year of Our Lord. They point forward to the time when He will come again.

Song: "Christ Shall Have Dominion"

(A choral group, a given class, or the pupils and audience may join to sing select verses of this song.)

ALL THREE ARE EMPTY

First Speaker: When Jesus was born in Bethlehem, His mother, Mary, wrapped Him in swaddling clothes and laid Him in a manger.

All: But the manger is empty now.

Second Speaker: After Jesus had been tried by the Jewish Sanhedrin and condemned by Pilate, the Roman soldiers led Jesus to Calvary and there they crucified Him.

All: But the cross is empty now.

Third Speaker: After Jesus had died, Joseph of Arimathea and Nicodemus took His body down from the cross and wrapped it in linen clothes. They buried Jesus in a new tomb and rolled a rock in front of His grave.

All: But His grave is empty now.

First Speaker: After Jesus arose from the grave, He ascended to heaven. There He sits at God's right hand, for all power and glory belong to Him.

Second Speaker: Before He rose to be with His Father, He gave us some work to do. He told us to preach the gospel to everyone, to tell them that "God so loved the world, that he gave his only begotten Son, that whosoever believeth in him should not perish, but have everlasting life."

Third Speaker: Jesus has promised that someday He will return. We must be ready for that great day. The second coming of Jesus will be different from the first.

First Speaker: He will not return as a babe in a manger.

Second Speaker: He will not need to die on a cross.

Third Speaker: He will not need to be buried again.

All: The manger, the cross, the grave—all three tell us of Jesus' love. They tell us of His victory—for all three are empty now.

HOW FAR IS IT TO BETHLEHEM?

First Speaker: How far is it to Bethlehem?

Second Speaker: Not very far.

First Speaker: Shall we find the stable-room
    Lit by a star?

Second Speaker: Can we see the little Child,
    Is He within?

First Speaker: If we lift the wooden latch,
    May we go in?

Second Speaker: May we stroke the creatures there,
    Ox, ass, or sheep?

First Speaker: May we peep like them and see
    Jesus asleep?

Second Speaker: If we touch His tiny hand,
    Will He awake?

First Speaker: Will He know we've come so far
    Just for His sake?

Together: Great kings have precious gifts,
    And we have naught;
Little smiles and little tears
    Are all we brought.

(Speakers hold out empty, open hands with palms up as they say the last line.)

Frances Chesterton, 1875-1938

AND THE WORD WAS MADE FLESH

First Speaker: Light looked down and beheld Darkness.
"Thither will I go," said Light.

Second Speaker: Peace looked down and beheld War.
"Thither will I go," said Peace.

Third Speaker: Love looked down and beheld Hatred.
"Thither will I go," said Love.

First Speaker: So came Light and shone.

Second Speaker: So came Peace and gave rest.

Third Speaker: So came Love and brought Life.

All: And the Word was made flesh.

(Make three posters or banners with the word **LIGHT** *on the first,* **PEACE** *on the second, and* **LOVE** *on the third. These should be carried by the appropriate speakers and raised when the part is spoken.)*

Laurence Housman

CHRISTMAS BELLS

(To be presented as an exercise by four children, each with a bell similar to those used by representatives of the Salvation Army at Christmas time. The children ring the bells as they enter, between verses, and as they exit.)

First Speaker: I heard the bells on Christmas Day
Their old familiar carols play,
   And wild and sweet
    The words repeat,
Of "Peace on earth, good will to men!"

Second Speaker: I thought how, as the day had come,
The belfries of all Christendom
   Had rolled along
    The unbroken song,
Of "Peace on earth, good will to men!"

Third Speaker: Till ringing, singing on its way,
The world revolved from night to day—
   A voice, a chime,
    A chant sublime,
Of "Peace on earth, good will to men!"

Fourth Speaker: And in despair I bowed my head;
"There is no peace on earth," I said,
   "For hate is strong
    And mocks the song
Of 'Peace on earth, good will to men!' "

All: Then pealed the bells more loud and deep:
"God is not dead; nor doth He sleep!
   The wrong shall fail,
    The right prevail,
With 'Peace on earth, good will to men!' "

(Variations: If no real bells are available for children to use in presenting the exercise, they could have colorful paper bells instead and simply swing them back and forth as they speak. The ringing sound could be provided by the bell in the church tower, the chimes of the church organ, or the ringing of a single bell at the side of the stage or platform. The poem could also be presented as a recitation by one child.)

Henry Wadsworth Longfellow

CHRISTMAS RYHTHMS

(an exercise for a reader and a rhythm band of primary children)

Reader: Long ago, at the very first Christmas, there was music. Angels sang and if you listened carefully you could hear many sounds of rhythm on the earth. Let's try to make some of the music that was heard at that time. Go back with me to a little village called Nazareth. Fathers are working. Mothers are cooking lunch. Children are playing in the streets. Suddenly one child hears a sound—like the music of a horse galloping along a stony road.

Sticks: Clippity Clop

Clippity Clop

Clippity, Clippity, Clippity Clop.

Reader: All the children rush to see the splendid rider. The horse is white and lifts his feet high as he runs. Fathers and mothers come out to see. The rider stops and blows upon a trumpet:

Horns: Da Dum

Da Dum

Da Dum, Da Dum, Da Dum.

Reader: Now all the people of the village gather around him. "People of Nazareth," he says, "I am a messenger of Caesar Augustus, your ruler. Caesar wants to know how many people live in his lands. So everyone must go back to the place where he was born, to be counted." Then the rider gets back on his horse and rides away. Listen to his horse gallop:

Sticks: Clippity Clop

Clippity Clop

Clippity, Clippity, Clippity Clop.

Reader: Now there is great confusion in the village for everyone must get ready to go to the place where he was born. Some people feel that they must board up their houses because they will be gone for a long time.

Drums: Let us hammer, hammer, hammer.

Sticks: Let us tap, tap, tap.

Drums: Let us hammer, hammer, hammer.

Sticks: Let us tap, tap, tap.

Reader: Now the houses are all safely boarded up. One woman says, "I will not go without my big brass pots for cooking."

Drums & Sticks: Get the pots.

Get the pots.

What a clang!

	What a bang!
	Get the pots.
Reader:	"We must take hay and grain for the donkeys," one man says, "for they will get very hungry and tired on this long journey."
Sand Blocks:	Bring the hay. Swish, swish.
	Bring the hay. Swish, swish.
	Pile it high
	Keep it dry
	Bring the hay. Swish, swish.
Reader:	"What about money?" one woman asks. "We must spend the nights in inns and we will have to pay for our rooms."
Triangles:	Here are our coins, hear them jingle.
	Here are our coins, hear them ring.
	Jingle and jangle, ringle and rangle—
	They bump in our pockets and sing.
Reader:	"We must take food for ourselves," a mother says, "for the journey is long. We must climb high mountains and go down steep paths and sometimes we may not be near a village where we can get food. Bring the dried beans."
Rattles:	Bring the beans as they rattle in the jar.
	Hear the beans as they rattle in the jar.
	When we're hungry, they'll taste good.
	We'll protect them as we should.
	Hear the beans as they rattle in the jar.
Reader:	Now, do we have everything? Then let's start on our journey. Though we will go to different places, we can begin together. We're on our way to Bethlehem.
	(The children march around playing their rhythm instruments as the pianist plays "O Come, All Ye Faithful.")
Reader:	At the fork in the road the neighbors who have been journeying together from Nazareth separate and each goes alone to the place of his birth as ordered by Caesar Augustus. Mary and Joseph travel for many days. It is lonely and the trip is long. At last, tired and weary, they arrive in Bethlehem. Joseph stops in front of a large inn. It will cost a great deal of money to stay here, but Mary is expecting a baby and he is worried that the trip has been too tiring for her. From inside the inn comes sounds of music and loud laughter.
Tambourines:	Laugh with the tambourine.
	Laugh with the tambourine.

	Forget tomorrow.
	Forget your sorrow
	And laugh with the tambourine.
Reader:	"I don't know how restful this place will be," Joseph says, "but at least you will be dry and warm and have a good soft bed to sleep on. Let's try it."
Sticks:	Knock, knock, knock,
	Knock, knock, knock.
	May we stay?
	We will pay.
	May we please? Knock, knock.
Reader:	But the innkeeper shakes his head. "I'm very sorry but we have no more room. We have been filled up for days. Try the inn down the road." Mary and Joseph trudge down the road to the next inn. Again, they hear sounds from inside.
Horns:	Attention, all soldiers! Da Dum.
	Line up for inspection! Da Dum.
Cymbals:	Are you in a straight line? Crash.
	Do your breastplates all shine? Crash.
	Do your swords look fine? Crash.
Horns:	Company, dismissed! Da Dum.
Reader:	"There seem to be many people in the courtyard," Joseph says, "but perhaps there is at least a small room and a bed. Let's see."
Sticks:	Knock, knock, knock,
	Knock, knock, knock.
	May we stay?
	We will pay.
	May we please? Knock, knock.
Reader:	"I'm very sorry, " the innkeeper says, "but all the soldiers who are doing the counting for Caesar are staying here. I'm so crowded I've even had to send my children away to stay with cousins. Perhaps one of the homes will take you in." Joseph thanks the innkeeper and they trudge down the road again. On the way they pass a small, neat home. "It looks quiet and restful," says Mary.
Sand Blocks:	Listen to the breeze in the trees. Swish, swish.
Bird Calls:	Listen to the birds. Coo, coo.
Sand Blocks:	It looks restful here. Swish, swish.

Bird Calls:	There is nothing to fear. Coo, coo.
Sand Blocks & Bird Calls:	Perhaps there's a place here for us.
Reader:	"Let's ask," Joseph says.
Sticks:	Knock, knock, knock,
	Knock, knock, knock.
	May we stay?
	We will pay.
	May we please? Knock, knock.
Reader:	But a nervous little woman comes to the door. "Oh, my goodness, no," she says. "No, no, no, it would never do. You see, I have cousins coming that I have never met. They are the wealthy side of the family. I think I see them coming now. Will you look at those fine camels! Yes, that's cousin Haseen."
Bells:	Ring, camel bells. Ring, ring.
Drums:	Drums keep the beat
	For the animals' feet,
	We must make a good show
	For our cousins, you know.
Bells:	Ring, camel bells. Ring, ring.
	Our arrival foretell. Ring, ring.
Reader:	The woman pleads: "Please, you must go. I have room only for these cousins." Sadly, Mary and Joseph move on. It is beginning to get dark and a cold wind is starting to blow. They trudge past a house with palm trees—
Sand Blocks:	Swish, swish.
Reader:	—past the inn with the soldiers—
Horn & Cymbals:	Da Dum. Da Dum. Crash.
Reader:	—until they stand again in front of the inn with the music and the laughter.
Tambourines:	Jingle, jingle.
Sticks:	Knock, knock, knock.
	Knock, knock, knock.
	There's no room in the town;
	We have looked all around.

>
> Have you *no* place,
>
> No place we could stay?

Reader: "Well," says the innkeeper, "there is the stable. You would at least be warm." Joseph sees Mary's face light up. The smell of fresh hay and the warm presence of gentle animals sound good after their long, tiring journey. The stable is large and quiet. Woolly sheep and friendly oxen move about softly. Mary nestles into the soft, warm hay. Joseph goes to shut the large wooden doors of the stable. Just before he closes them he looks out over the town of Bethlehem. Lights are going out in some of the homes. From the inn loud noise continues to rise. Let's all use our instruments to make the sounds he might have heard.

(The piano plays, "O Little Town of Bethlehem" as all the children play their instruments.)

Reader: Then Joseph shuts the large wooden doors tightly and all is still.

(All the children sing the first verse of "Silent Night" softly.)

Reader: In the stillness of the night, the baby Jesus was born. Angels sang at His birth—the most beautiful music in the world. Let's imagine that we are there on that first Christmas night. Let's imagine that we are marching around the manger where Jesus lay. Let's play our instruments softly and sing.

Song: "Away in a Manger"

Reader: On Christmas Eve, the stable was quiet and peaceful with angel songs and kneeling shepherds, but in another place things were different. Herod was the ruling king and in his mighty palace there was no quiet and there was no peace. Inside the servants were hurrying about doing Herod's bidding. Herod is in an angry mood tonight. The three wise men have come to see him—to ask him where they can find the new King. Herod beats his fist on the table. To himself he says:

Sticks:
>
> I am the king.
>
> I am the king.
>
> No one can rule the land
>
> The way that Herod can.
>
> I am the king.
>
> I am the king.

Reader: But to the wise men he says:

Triangles:
>
> A baby is born, you say?
>
> A baby is born, you say?
>
> Find him and let me know
>
> So that with you I may go.
>
> I would see this new king.
>
> I would see this new king.

Reader: After they are gone, Herod rumbles (drums roll) and he beats his fist on the wall (drum beats).

Sticks:
    I am the king.

    I am the king.

    No one can rule this land

    The way that Herod can.

    I am the king.

    I am the king.

Reader: "Bring me my money and jewels to count," he orders.

Bells:
    Listen to my money, jingle, jingle.

    Listen to my money, jingle, jingle.

    I could buy anything—

    Houses, carriages, and rings.

    Listen to my money, jingle, jingle.

Reader: But after a while King Herod got bored with counting his money. And still he was angry and worried. "Everyone come in here," he shouted. "Play as loud as you can for me so I will forget my troubles."

(All instruments play as loudly and discordantly as possible for a short time.)

Reader: But Herod's troubles did not go away for he was a king of war and hate; and the new King, the Lord Jesus, was a King of love and peace. There was a lot of music and rhythm on that first Christmas Eve. Some was noisy and harsh. Some was soft and beautiful. Some would make you happy and some would make you cry. Let's end by singing a song of joy and gladness for the Savior who came to earth on Christmas Eve.

Song: "Oh, How I Love Jesus"

(Sticks play a rhythmic march as children leave the platform.)

Adapted from a Christmas program
written by Dorothy Semeyn and given at
Arcadia Christian Reformed Church,
Grand Rapids.

CHRISTMAS PROPHECY

(Speaker one stands at the left of the platform and holds a poster with the words IN THE BEGINNING WAS THE WORD.)

Speaker One: The Gospel of John opens with these words: "In the beginning was the Word, and the Word was with God, and the Word was God. . . . All things were made by him; and without him was not anything made that was made." These verses tell us that Jesus lived with God the Father long before He came to earth to be our Savior.

(Speaker two stands next to speaker one and holds a poster with the words: GOD'S PROMISE TO ADAM AND EVE.)

Speaker Two: Shortly after Adam and Eve fell into sin, God gave to them the first promise of Christ's coming in the words of Genesis 3:15: "And I will put enmity between thee and the woman, and between thy seed and her seed; it shall bruise thy head, and thou shalt bruise his heel." This first prophecy foretells that Jesus will win the victory over Satan.

(Speaker three stands next to speaker two and holds a poster with the words: GOD'S PROMISE TO ABRAHAM.)

Speaker Three: God established the covenant of grace with Abraham in Genesis 12:3: "And I will bless them that bless thee, and curse him that curseth thee: and in thee shall all families of the earth be blessed." We too have been blessed because God kept His promise to Abraham and sent Jesus to be born as our Savior.

(Speaker four holds a poster with the words: THE PSALMS TELL OF JESUS' RESURRECTION.)

Speaker Four: King David, who was an ancestor of Jesus, wrote in Psalm 16:10: "For thou wilt not leave my soul in hell; neither wilt thou suffer thine Holy One to see corruption." Long before Jesus was born His victory over death and the grave was already foretold.

(Speaker five holds a poster with the words: ISAIAH FORETOLD MANY THINGS ABOUT CHRIST.)

Speaker Five: The prophet Isaiah foretold many things about the coming Messiah. In Isaiah 7:14 we read: "Therefore the Lord himself shall give you a sign; Behold, a virgin shall conceive, and bear a son, and shall call his name Immanuel." And in Isaiah 9:6 we read: "For unto us a child is born, unto us a son is given: and the government shall be upon his shoulder: and his name shall be called Wonderful, Counsellor, The mighty God, The everlasting Father, The Prince of Peace.

(Speaker six holds a poster with the words: MICAH PROPHESIES WHERE JESUS WILL BE BORN.)

Speaker Six: When the wise men followed the star in search of the Savior, they came to Jerusalem and asked King Herod, "Where is he who has been born king of the Jews?" Herod called the chief priests and the scribes, and inquired of them where the Christ was to be born. They told him what the prophet

Micah had foretold hundreds of years before: "But thou, Bethlehem Ephratah, though thou be little among the thousands of Judah, yet out of thee shall he come forth unto me that is to be ruler in Israel; whose goings forth have been from of old, from everlasting."

(Speaker seven holds a poster with the words: AND THE WORD WAS MADE FLESH AND DWELT AMONG US.)

Speaker Seven: The story of Christmas really began in eternity. Before the world was created and time began, God the Father designated that His Son would be the Savior of the world. And when the right time came, God sent His Son, born of a woman, that He might save sinful mankind, that He might save you and me. This is the story of Christmas.

All: "And the Word was made flesh and dwelt among us, . . . full of grace and truth."

IN THE TOWN

Joseph: Take heart, the journey's ended:
            I see the twinkling lights,
        Where we shall be befriended
            On this the night of nights.

Mary: Now praise the Lord that led us
            So safe unto the town,
        Where men will feed and bed us,
            And I can lay me down.

Joseph: Look yonder, wife, look yonder!
            An hostelry I see.
        Where travelers that wander
            Will very welcome be.

Mary: The house is tall and stately,
            The door stands open thus;
        Yet, husband, I fear greatly
            That inn is not for us.

Joseph: God save you, gentle master!
            Your littlest room indeed
        With plainest walls of plaster
            Tonight will serve our need.

Host: For lordlings and for ladies
            I've lodging and to spare:
        For you and yonder maid is
            No closet anywhere.

Joseph: Take heart, take heart, sweet Mary,
            Another inn I spy,
        Whose host will not be chary
            To let us easy lie.

Mary: Oh, aid me, I am ailing.
            My strength is nearly gone;
        I feel my limbs are failing.
            And yet we must go on.

Joseph: God save you, hostess, kindly!
            I pray you, house my wife.
        Who bears beside me blindly
            The burden of her life.

Hostess: My guests are rich men's daughters
            And sons, I'd have you know!
        Seek out the poorer quarters
            Where ragged people go.

Mary: In all the lighted city
            Where rich men welcome win,
        Will not one house for pity
            Take two poor strangers in?

Joseph: Good woman, I implore you,
    Afford my wife a bed.

Hostess: Nay, nay, I've nothing for you
    Except the cattle-shed.

Mary: Then gladly in the manger
    Our bodies we will house,
Since men tonight are stranger
    Than oxen are and cows.

Joseph: Take heart, take heart, sweet Mary,
    The cattle are our friends:
Lie down, lie down, sweet Mary,
    For here our journey ends.

Mary: Now praise the Lord that found me
    This shelter in the town.
Where I with friends around me
    May lay my burden down.

Song: "Silent Night"

Adapted from a fifteenth-century French carol

Part Six
CHORAL READINGS

CHRISTMAS EVERYWHERE

(to be presented as a choral reading by a speaking choir)

All:	Everywhere, everywhere, Christmas tonight!
Solo- Light Voice:	Christmas in lands of fir-tree and pine,
Solo- Dark Voice:	Christmas in lands of palm-tree and vine,
Group- Light Voices:	Christmas where snow-peaks stand solemn and white,
Group- Dark Voices:	Christmas where cornfields lie sunny and bright,
All:	Everywhere, everywhere, Christmas tonight!
Group- Light Voices:	Christmas where children are hopeful and gay, Christmas where old men are patient and gray,
Group- Dark Voices:	Christmas where peace, like a dove in its flight, Broods o'er brave men in the thick of the fight.
All:	Everywhere, everywhere, Christmas tonight!
Solo- Light Voice:	For the Christ child who comes is the Master of all, No palace too great and no cottage too small; The angels who welcome Him sing from the height,
Group- Light Voices:	"In the city of David, a king in His might." Everywhere, everywhere, Christmas tonight!
Group- Dark Voices:	Then let every heart keep its Christmas within,
1st Solo- Dark Voice:	Christ's pity for sorrow,
2nd Solo- Dark Voice:	Christ's hatred for sin,
3rd Solo- Dark Voice:	Christ's care for the weakest,
4th Solo- Dark Voice:	Christ's courage for right,
5th Solo- Dark Voice:	Christ's dread of the darkness,

6th Solo-
    Dark Voice: Christ's love of the light.

Group-
    Dark Voices: Everywhere, everywhere, Christmas tonight!

Group-
    Light Voices: So the stars of the midnight which compass us round
                        Shall see a strange glory, and hear a sweet sound,
                        And cry,

Solo-
    Light Voice: "Look! the earth is aflame with delight,
                        O sons of the morning, rejoice at the sight."

All: Everywhere, everywhere, Christmas tonight!

                                          Phillips Brooks, 1835-1893

INCARNATE LOVE

(To be presented as a choral reading by a speaking choir including three light and three dark voices)

Solo-
   Light Voice: Love came down at Christmas.

Duet-
   Light Voices: Love all lovely, Love divine;

Solo-
   Light Voice: Love was born at Christmas,

Duet-
   Light Voices: Star and angels gave the sign.

Duet-
   Dark Voices: Worship we the Godhead,

Solo-
   Dark Voice: Love incarnate, Love divine;

Duet-
   Dark Voices: Worship we our Jesus:

Solo-
   Dark Voice: But wherewith for sacred sign?

Duet-
   One Light,
   One Dark   Love shall be our token,
   Voice: Love be yours and love be mine,

Sextet-
   Three Light,
   Three Dark   Love to God and all men,
   Voices: Love for plea and gift and sign.

                             Christina Rossetti

LET US GO EVEN UNTO BETHLEHEM

Solo Voice: The Christmas story leads us to the little town of Bethlehem for long ago the prophet Micah wrote:

Speaking Choir: But thou, Bethlehem Ephratah, though thou be little among the thousands of Judah, yet of thee shall he come forth unto me that is to be the ruler in Israel; whose goings forth have been from of old, from everlasting.

Solo Voice: Bethlehem is sometimes called the City of David for it was the place where David was born,

Two Voices: The place where he lived and kept his father's sheep.

Solo Voice: When God told Samuel, the prophet, to anoint another king in the place of Saul, He sent Samuel to Jesse, the Bethlehemite. After Samuel had seen all of Jesse's older sons, he asked Jesse if there was still another. Jesse replied that there was one younger son, David, who was keeping the sheep.

Two Voices: It was David whom God had chosen to be king over Israel and Samuel anointed David in Bethlehem.

Solo Voice: But Bethlehem filled its most important place in history on that first Christmas night when the angels proclaimed:

Speaking Choir: Fear not; for, behold, I bring you good tidings of great joy, which shall be to all people. For unto you is born this day in the city of David a Savior, which is Christ the Lord. And this shall be a sign unto you; Ye shall find the babe wrapped in swaddling clothes, lying in a manger.

Solo Voice: The herald angel's proclamation has been made. Suddenly there is a heavenly host:

Trio of Voices: The morning stars sing together, And all the sons of God shout for joy.

Solo Voice: Then the heavenly chorus sounds forth,

Speaking Choir: Glory to God in the highest, and on earth peace, good will toward men.

Solo Voice: And it came to pass, as the angels were gone away from them into heaven, the shepherds said one to another,

Trio of Voices: Let us now go even unto Bethlehem, and see this thing which is come to pass, which the Lord hath made known unto us.

Song: "O Little Town of Bethlehem"

CHRISTMAS

(to be presented as a choral reading by a speaking choir)

Solo-
Light Voice: Good people all, this Christmas time,
Consider well and bear in mind
What our good God for us has done,

Duet-
Light Voices: In sending His beloved Son.
With virgin Mary we should pray
To God with love this Christmas Day:

Trio-
Light Voices: In Bethlehem upon that morn
There was a blessed Messiah born.

Trio-
Dark Voices: Near Bethlehem did shepherds keep
Their flocks of lambs and feeding sheep;
To whom God's angels did appear,
Which put the shepherds in great fear.

Trio-
Light Voices: "Prepare and go," the angels said,
"To Bethlehem, be not afraid:
For there you'll find, this happy morn,
A princely babe, sweet Jesus born."

Solo-
Dark Voice: With thankful heart and joyful mind,
The shepherds went the babe to find.
And as God's angel had foretold,
They did our Savior Christ behold.

Trio-
Dark Voices: Within a manger he was laid,
And by His side the virgin maid.
Attending on the Lord of life,
Who came to earth to end all strife.

Song: "While Shepherds Watched Their Flocks by Night"

Selected verses from a traditional Irish carol

A SONG OF SALVATION

This choral reading, based on selections from the Messianic Psalms, could be given effectively with organ music used as an introduction and at transition points in the rendition of the choral work.

Leader: In the beginning God created the heaven and the earth.... God created man in his own image.... And God saw everything that he had made, and, behold, *it was very good*.

Speech Choir: O Lord our Lord, how excellent is thy name in all the earth!

Who has set thy glory above the heavens....

When I consider thy heavens, the work of thy fingers, the moon and the stars, which thou hast ordained;

What is man, that thou art mindful of him? And the son of man, that thou visitest him?

For thou hast made him a little lower than the angels, and hast crowned him with glory and honor.

Thou madest him to have dominion over the works of thy hands;

Thou hast put all things under his feet:

All sheep and oxen, yea, and the beasts of the field; the fowl of the air, and the fish of the sea, and whatsoever passeth through the paths of the seas.

O Lord our Lord, how excellent is thy name in all the earth!

Leader: But man rebelled against God, and earned the wages of sin—death. In Adam *all* died: *all* have sinned and come short of the glory of God.

Speech Choir: The fool hath said in his heart, There is no God.

They are corrupt, they have done abominable works,

There is none that doeth good.

The Lord looked down from heaven upon the children of men, to see if there were any that did understand, and seek God.

They are *all* gone aside;

They are *all* together become filthy:

There is none that doeth good,

No, not one!

Leader: "But the Lord is merciful and gracious, slow to anger, and plenteous in mercy.... He hath not dealt with us after our sins; nor rewarded us according to our iniquities." God provided a Savior for His people—His only begotten Son. Jesus Christ, the God-Man, was the only One who was able to pay the price of our redemption.

Speech Choir: Sacrifice and offering thou didst not desire....

Burnt offering and sin offering hast thou not required.

Then said I, Lo, I come: in the volume of the book it is written of me,

	I delight to do thy will, O my God: yea, thy law is within my heart.
Leader:	Christ lived a sinless life for us on earth; He fulfilled the perfect law of God. He also made the supreme sacrifice for our sins through His suffering and death on the cross.
Speech Choir:	But I am a worm, and no man; a reproach of men, and despised of the people.
	All they that see me laugh me to scorn;
	They shoot out the lip, they shake the head, saying, He trusted on the Lord that he would deliver him: let him deliver him, seeing he delighted in him....
	I am poured out like water, and all my bones are out of joint: my heart is like wax.... My strength is dried up like a potsherd; and my tongue cleaveth to my jaws;
	And thou hast brought me into the dust of death....
	I may tell all my bones: they look and stare upon me. They part my garments among them, and cast lots upon my vesture.
	My God, my God, why hast thou forsaken me?
Leader:	God heard the agonized prayers and cries of His beloved Son in Gethsemane and at Calvary.
Speech Choir:	In my distress I called upon the Lord, and cried unto my God....
	Then the earth shook and trembled;
	The foundations also of the hills moved and were shaken....
	He bowed the heavens also, and came down: and darkness was under his feet....
	He delivered me from my strong enemy....
	He delivered me, because he delighted in me....
	Therefore my heart is glad, and my glory rejoiceth: my flesh also shall rest in hope.
	For thou wilt not leave my soul in hell; neither wilt thou suffer thine Holy One to see corruption.
Leader:	Christ arose from the grave a Victor over death and hell. He ascended into heaven where He reigns as the eternal King.
Speech Choir:	Lift up your heads, O ye gates; even lift them up, ye everlasting doors;
	And the King of glory shall come in.
	Who is this King of glory?
	The Lord strong and mighty, the Lord mighty in battle.
	Lift up your heads, O ye gates; even lift them up, ye everlasting doors;
	And the King of glory shall come in.
	Who is this King of glory?
	The Lord of hosts, he is the King of glory!

Leader: "The Lord said to my Lord, Sit thou at my right hand, until I make thine enemies thy footstool." When the last of God's children have come to Him in faith and repentance, the end of time will come and "the Lord himself shall descend from heaven with a shout, with the voice of the archangel, and with the trump of God." Christ's eternal kingdom will be established.

Speech Choir: O sing unto the Lord a new song; for he hath done marvelous things:

His right hand, and his holy arm, hath gotten him the victory!

The Lord hath made known his salvation: his righteousness hath he openly shewed in the sight of the heathen. . . .

Let the sea roar, and the fullness thereof; the world, and they that dwell therein.

Let the floods clap their hands: let the hills be joyful together before the Lord!

For he cometh to judge the earth: With righteousness shall he judge the world, and the people with equity.

Leader: Before Jesus, the Son of David, every knee will bow, and every tongue will confess Him to be Lord of lords and King of kings. He shall reign for ever and ever.

Speech Choir:
Praise ye the Lord!
Praise God in the sanctuary:
Praise him in the firmament of his power.
Praise him for his mighty acts:
Praise him according to his excellent greatness.
Praise him with the sound of the trumpet:
Praise him with the psaltery and harp.
Praise him with the timbrel and dance:
Praise him with stringed instruments and organs.
Praise him upon the loud cymbals:
Praise him upon the high sounding cymbals.
Let every thing that hath breath praise the Lord.
PRAISE YE THE LORD!